Be BOLD

You Were Never Meant To Fit In

Compiled By Kyra Schaefer

As You Wish Publishing, LLC
Connect@asyouwishpublishing.com

ISBN: 978-1-951131-54-8

Library of Congress Control Number: 2023900124

Table of Contents

CHAPTER

Surviving Death
By Rose Bourassa

Rose Bourassa had a distinguished career as a procurement specialist. Away from work, she has worn many hats: mother, grandmother, student, and teacher. Recently retired, she has become an international bestselling author and serves her community by volunteering with her local library and, most recently, the local Relay for Life Team. She holds board offices with both groups. She strives to learn something new every day to keep her mind sharp and interact with her grandkids to keep her young at heart. She is currently preparing for a second career as an evidential medium.

You can contact Rose via email at Remnick@aol.com.

Chapter 1

Surviving Death

By Rose Bourassa

W E HAVE ALL ENCOUNTERED the death of someone we knew and loved in our lives. Understanding and processing that death is something different.

My mother had a miscarriage sometime after my sister was born. But I did not know what that meant nor understood her grief.

My first real encounter with death happened when I was ten years old. I vividly recall my aunt sitting on my bed one night. She was telling me goodbye. Her earthly time was up, and she needed to leave. Moments later, the phone rang, and my parents had to hurry out of the house. Later in the morning, they would tell us that my aunt had died hours earlier. But I already knew that.

They didn't believe me when I told them that she was in my room saying goodbye. After all, I was just a kid, and I must have dreamed it when I heard their phone conversation. Because I was "too young." I was not allowed to attend the funeral either. It was probably for the best, anyway. What did I understand about death? I understood nothing at all at that point in my life.

Death seemed to wrap its arms around me during my high school years. So many of my classmates died during our formative years. Drugs were making the scene, and one of my classmates was high one night and decided to go swimming in the school pool. Unfortunately, he chose to take a high dive into an empty pool.

Another classmate had a part-time job at a drive-through dairy and was killed in a robbery, while several others lost their lives in auto accidents. My neighbor, who was a year ahead of me in school, died of a brain aneurysm while driving. Still, another teenage neighbor died in a scuba diving accident.

How does one lose so many friends in three years and not be affected by it? I am still trying to figure that out. Many more classmates lost their lives in the first five years after high school.

I may not have known them all, but I was sad to hear the news. One of those lost was my childhood best friend. Somehow we lost contact during our senior year in school. She died of leukemia two years after graduation. To this day, I still regret not reaching out after we graduated. Another elementary schoolmate died execution-style in a drug deal gone bad.

By the time I turned twenty-one, I had lost over a dozen people, most of whom were my age!

Somewhere in my early adulthood, I lost my Great Aunt Mary. I remember she had a medical issue, and my mother complained that her kids were responsible for her death. They should have left her alone and let her live her life out, but they wanted her to get a corrective surgery so she would live longer. Well, we all know that didn't work out too well. At the viewing, my mom was taking pictures. Seriously Mom? Who needs pictures of someone lying in a coffin? Not me. And she did that touchy, feely thing I can't do either. I vividly remember her saying how my aunt had plastic under her clothes and why she had to have it. It turned my stomach.

A few years after I married, my grandmother took ill. It was a most trying time. The arguments about her care between my mother and her siblings were so out of hand. I always seemed to be stuck in the middle of them. When she passed, the discontent amongst the family seemed to distract from the grief. It should have been a time to come together, but it wasn't.

On viewing night, there was a big row in the mortuary parking lot over my brother's ex-wife being there. I felt like the arguing was never going to stop. Let it be already! There was no time for grieving when you were trying to play peacemaker.

Then the story of the night Grandma died and who was with her when she passed changed a dozen times. When I got the call that she had passed, I rushed to my parent's home. Grandma was still there in her hospital bed. As I looked at her, I saw her and God together. Boy, was she giving him heck for everything wrong on earth. Was it my vivid imagination, or was I catching a glimpse of the other side?

My father was with Grandma when she passed; Mom had gone to bed. But to my mother's story, she had barely stepped towards the bedroom. Or was it two steps? Three? Four? I heard them all! Guess it depends on which version you heard.

When my son was barely three years old, my father died. It was a hard night for me. He had been in and out of hospitals for months. The day he died, he was transferred from ICU in the local hospital to a regular room in another. We talked by phone that night. I told him I loved him, but I'm not sure he heard me. A few hours later, I received the call he had passed. I rushed to meet my mom and younger brother at the hospital. We were ushered into a room, not allowed to be with my father. We asked the staff if they would contact the local Catholic church to have a priest come and administer the last rites. They looked at us like we were crazy. Every request we made seemed to fall on deaf ears. We were allowed into my father's room when a priest finally arrived. I couldn't believe that they had not prepared him for our visit. It should have been illegal to see what condition he was left in. Apparently, in this hospital, they have no respect for the dead.

When I arrived home several hours later, I found my three-year-old in my bed, keeping my side warm for me. As I cuddled with him and my husband, I cried. I explained to my son that his grandpa had died and why Mommy was sad. Then my sweet young man hugged me tight and said, "It's okay, Mommy. I still have another grandpa."

Dad's funeral was the first I had any part in helping to plan. After making a million phone calls to spread the word, we went to the mortuary to make arrangements. We knew the owners, and they knew I had a small child, so they gave me a book on how to approach funerals with young children. It nicely explained the closing of the casket before the funeral service. My son decided that his job was to close the casket.

The morning of the funeral, we arrived at the mortuary early to spend our last moments with Dad. Standing at the casket, Dad looked remarkably peaceful and ever so handsome. My son watched my mother touch Dad's hands as she said her final goodbyes. I'm not too fond of that touchy-feeling thing she does. My son then wanted to touch his hands too. I permitted him to do so, but he insisted I touch him first. Oh great! Now, what do I do? Pass on my phobia or touch a dead person? It took every ounce of strength, but I felt my father's hands as did my son. And then he proclaimed to the funeral director it was his job to close the box. So they helped him close it.

You're a mom and need to be strong, and you aren't strong if you're crying. Throughout the entire process of losing my father, I never cried other than the night he died. I did not want to create a scenario where I was perceived as weak in dealing with death, especially while having a small child.

Over the next six months, both of my father's brothers and one of his sisters would die. My father's family tree was rapidly being trimmed.

There was a period of time when no one in the family died. That ended when my sister lost her son in childbirth. It was a challenging time for the family, especially my mom. Mom has lost her firstborn child as well. We were allowed to meet with the baby privately to say hello and goodbye simultaneously. I will never forget that painful look on my mother's face as she held her grandson and cried. She never got to meet her daughter. She never held her. She never got to say hello and goodbye. All those bottled-up emotions were now on the table, and I felt helpless to do anything to comfort her.

A few years later, my mom's brother died. That would be the start of another round of loss. Every time we turned around, there was yet another funeral to attend. Where were the weddings and the births? They were so few and far between. It indeed seemed this cycle of death was never-ending.

We would lose two more uncles before we lost Mom. Mom fell and broke her hip one Sunday morning. That was the beginning of the end. Eighteen months later, I received a call that she had a heart attack in the convalescent home and had been rushed to the hospital. (They didn't tell me on that call that she was left unattended and had fallen. Doctors believed that the fall triggered the heart attack.) Mom was 87 at the time. I was her power of attorney. I knew what her wishes were. The most challenging line I ever spoke in my life was to the emergency room doctor. "She is DNR." He either didn't hear me or chose not to hear me because he continued to explain the procedures he wanted to perform on my mother. I now had to repeat myself loudly and firmly. *"She's DNR."*

A few days later would be my birthday. Instead of preparing to celebrate, I told my mom I had everything under control and it was okay for her to leave us. She'd raised her family well, and we would all be fine without her here to watch over us.

Her children took turns telling her it was okay to leave us. I prayed all week silently for her not to die on my birthday. On Friday at 5 pm, the doctor told me he was releasing her to go home to hospice care. Seriously? How did he expect me to get hospice arranged on a Friday night after hours? Somehow I managed to get him to allow her to stay until Monday when I could make proper arrangements. She died peacefully Sunday morning.

While dealing with everything for Mom, my senior dog, Penny, was experiencing health issues. She had a growing tumor on her chest and another on her heart. Our vet told us he could be in our pockets deep to treat her, but the result would not change. We were going to lose our girl. We knew it was just a matter of time before she would leave us too. Just before Easter, we made the hard decision to let her go. Mom hadn't been gone but a few weeks, and now we were going to say goodbye to our girl. As hard as it was to lose Mom, it was harder to lose our Penny. I cried when Mom passed, but I had a total breakdown when we said goodbye to Penny. It was hard to walk into the vet's office with a dog and know we would leave with only her leash and collar. It still brings a tear to my eye when I think about that day.

March and April were terrible months for losing the ones we loved.

In early July, I received a call about a dear friend; she was being taken to the hospital. I should come. I was her power of attorney, and the hospital thought I should be there. When I arrived, my friend was surprised to see me there. I asked her what was going on. A nurse walked into the room, and my friend asked the nurse to explain it to me. "Talk to the nurse and then go home to your family. You don't need to be here. I'm fine." But she wasn't okay. She had cancer in several places in her body, and it was progressing. The hospital asked for copies of my Power of Attorney. Since I did not have them with me, I told them I would fax the documents when I got home. The following day I received a call from the hospital. My friend was unresponsive, and they wanted to do some scans but needed permission, which I granted. When I arrived at the hospital, the results were back in. She'd had a significant brain bleed. She was not expected to wake up, and I needed to make arrangements for hospice care. They anticipated she could last from three to seven days—time to make decisions again.

One thing I was sure of; I needed a Catholic priest to see her before she was transferred anywhere. Thankfully, the hospital chaplain was a remarkable man who found a priest for me. He was indeed a blessing from the moment we met.

The priest arrived on Saturday morning and anointed her. An hour later, she was transferred to hospice care at a nearby facility. I followed the ambulance and watched as they got her comfy in her room. I could hear her in my mind telling me, "This place is a dump! Not my choice of where I want to be!" I stayed for a while and decided I should go home. Before leaving, I stopped at the nurse's station to ensure they had my cell phone number in case they needed me. I mentioned to the nurse that my friend was not happy with her surroundings. Later that night, I received a call from the hospitalist doctor. She had just come from my friend's room and wanted me to know she was now unresponsive. She tried to understand how we'd had a conversation when she could not speak before being transferred. She did not appreciate our ability to converse without speaking aloud. (As it would turn out, I wouldn't understand it till ten years later myself.)

Here I was on a Saturday late afternoon, thinking about how the next week would go. Doctors told me brain bleed would take her life in three to seven days. Mom had passed barely three months earlier. My Lexi girl two months earlier. Did I have the strength and wisdom for another person to die? I was not sure I could get through another week of hospital visits. This time I would be on my own. She had no living family. I was it. But she was part of my family. My kids called her "Aunt." She had been part of all our family celebrations long before I married and had children. I didn't have to deal with a week at all. A few hours after telling the doctor we had a mental conversation, she called to tell me my friend died peacefully in her sleep. I knew she disliked the facility but dying to get out of it? Thus the funeral planning began again.

Three deaths in early 2011. When my friend died, I hadn't had time to square away everything for my mom. Luckily, this was the last death I had to deal with till 2014.

There were four significant deaths in my life starting in 2014. These deaths would shape the future of my life, although I did not know that at the time.

Death #1 was my son. He lost his life in a tragic auto accident the week before Thanksgiving and his dad's birthday. It was indeed a trying time. The suddenness of his passing and the questions about the accident that would never be answered still haunt me. We already had plans for a big family get-together for Thanksgiving. Instead, we would gather, without the traditional turkey, and eat the leftover funeral reception food. My son's chair would remain empty at the table. My heart would forever be broken.

One month later, I would unknowingly begin my journey into the world of mediumship. I would start my quest to search for and understand life after death. This quest would serve as my coping method to deal with my son's passing. I was fortunate to have a wonderful friend who was a developing medium. She became my guide and mentored me in the spirit world.

Death #2 came a few years later. Another dear friend, who had given me power of attorney for her medical care, had taken ill. Why did people want me as their medical power of attorney? Because they wanted someone who would understand when it was time to pull the plug and do it. It's not like I enjoyed the job, but it was not a job to like but rather to respect and honor that decision and act on it when it came. It took someone special to step up and make those hard calls. I was that person.

I had spirit world experience under my belt when I was called to this duty. My friend and I discussed what life on the other side might be like. She was tasked with finding my son and kicking his behind for leaving us as he did. She relished that assignment. It was my honor to spend her final hours with her when she passed.

The experience of feeling the presence of her family reunion in the room was overwhelming. Each soul that entered passed through me with a wave of unconditional love so warm and bright I was sure everyone in the room was seeing it too. It was an experience I will never forget.

My next significant death experience would be that of my husband. He was diagnosed with stage 4 lung cancer and given 18 months at best. He was never a big believer in the spirit world. There were moments when he believed, but they didn't last long. If ever there was a true skeptic, he was it. During his last days, he called "the party on the ceiling" to my attention. My thoughts were elsewhere, and I replied, "What?" He waved his hand at me and said, "You're supposed to know this stuff!" That would not be the last time he referred to the party, but it made me much more aware of the spirits coming to my home to visit him. Some of them would arrive in the middle of the night and very politely ring the doorbell to be sure I was aware they were there. Life with the spirits was engaging in his last few days. I'd spent most of my nights sleeping in the recliner next to him, but for some reason, I slept in my bed the night he passed. He had decided he didn't want me in the room when he left us and waited for the night I slept in our room. Like everything else he did, he died on his terms. As heartbreaking as it was to lose my husband, I took comfort in knowing he had reunited with our son, and now he was a believer in the spirit world!

When my spirit world mentor died nine months after my husband, my world came to a screeching halt. The shock was unbearable and threw me into a tailspin, and I thought I would never recover. She was ill with covid and had underlying conditions, but never in my wildest dreams did I believe she would lose the battle. She was there for me when my son died. She was my spirit world teacher and mentor. The morning after my friend died, she was the one I called to share my experience with. Through my husband's illness, she was there for me with loving support. That day, I lost a beloved friend, an un-biological sister, and a spirit world confidant, a friend who supported me on so many different levels of my life. She had been my lifeboat since 2014, and now she was gone.

There must be a coping mechanism in life for losing everyone you love. I often joked with new friends not to get close to me as everyone I love dies. The reality is I know where they all are. They didn't leave me and are as near as my thoughts. They are with me consistently; I hear them puttering around the house. I can feel their touch at times.

None of this diminishes the pain of losing them in the physical world, but it does warm the heart, knowing they live close by and I will see them again.

What is the meaning of losing all these people? Is there a purpose behind this? A lesson to be learned?

Of course, there is. Do I understand it all? Not totally, but I will in time. Each death in my life was different, and a lesson was learned from each experience.

Shortly after my son died, I was called upon to help friends deal with the loss of their son. Losing my son had taught me that I was to help other grieving parents work through the loss of their child, to share with them that there is life after death and their child is close at hand, and to deliver messages of love from the other side. Did I realize that spirit was calling on me to be of service? Not at that moment, but I later learned that was the beginning of my calling to serve the spirit world.

Losing my husband to cancer taught me that cancer should not win. I am needed to help find a cure, and I set out to do so by joining my local Relay for Life team, raising funds, and drawing awareness of the need for improved cancer research for the cure and support for families in need. My mediumship comes into play when I meet parents who have lost a child to this dreaded disease and need to know their child is alive and well on the other side.

Losing my best friend in this world taught me that spirit has a plan for me, and she was now needed on the other side to help complete the program and be the leader of my spirit guide team. She, with my husband and son, will be there to help guide me as I navigate this life and carry out the duties spirit had assigned to me.

Death is not something I fear in life. In its quirky way, every death I experience is a life lesson that helps me survive death. An experience that enriches my life and enables me to serve others in need. When it is my turn to leave this plane, I hope to do so with dignity and honor and be remembered for the good works I did while on this earth. I trust that a lesson in surviving death will be learned for those I leave behind.

CHAPTER

Two

Trauma Created Healing
By Crystal Camp-Kravtsov

Crystal is a rebellious free spirit at heart who marches to her own drum while audaciously moving forward from the trauma that tried to consume her life. What is this life for? Crystal's head was full of endless thoughts directing her away from life's beauty, all in an attempt to keep her from exploring this journey of life. Told she was a fish out of water due to non-compliance with following some guided rules set in place by a bunch of imbeciles who thought rules would suit everyone. One day, while checking in on her thoughts, she wondered if she was supposed to be here in this silly, chaotic world, and it turned out she was the one that signed up to take this journey through a life of exploration in finding self. An exploration of helping to heal others' trauma while seamlessly trying to recover from her own. She is strong and has been known to blow others away with her willingness to serve others selflessly by offering guidance through healing sessions. Her light shines bright for all to see, even for the ones in the dark who have tried to keep the light from shining through her.

How to reach Crystal

Facebook- The Gifted Psychic Healer
Email- crystal@thegiftedpsychichealer.com
Website- thegiftedpsychichealer.com

Chapter 2

Trauma Created Healing

By Crystal Camp-Kravtsov

P ICK YOURSELF UP, CRYSTAL. She hears the whispers softly coming through her ears. Feeling unmotivated and unwilling, she trusts this voice and lifts her head to find no one there as this voice comes from her inner self, the higher self. That intuitive feeling of knowing kicked in for her as she became aware of this voice. This voice was different from the other one that was always telling her negative stuff and sending beliefs out to her mind that she knew deep inside were untrue. The two voices are distinguished by sensations felt in her gut, a form of truth testing through the nervous system of her body. Later on, after reading a spiritual help book, *The Power of Now*, she is able to help her ego become friends with her intuition. Working together, as Alan Watts says, so when her ego is acting out of flight or fight mode when it's unnecessary, her intuition can remind her ego that they are safe and begin to reframe the scenario to a more positive one. This method has worked many times for Crystal, allowing her to continue down the path of exploring and healing herself.

How did I get here?

Some of us are born straight into traumatic situations, and immediately we begin to adapt to coping with stress, fear, and the unknown. Love is smothered in shame, guilt, and fear, creating quite the concoction to build up in one's brain. This event starts while the baby is in the womb, and it will begin to take on stressors that the mother is experiencing while pregnant and become encoded into the baby's genetic makeup. Another mind-expanding scenario is that, as a baby, we will come into this world with stored lineage traumas. Meaning that the experiences our ancestors endured become encoded within our DNA until someone else comes through to heal it. When we begin healing ourselves from the trauma, we, in turn, heal our ancestors and release them from it. The healing travels back up through the lineage's point of origin. Lucky me, I chose a heavy trauma-filled family to come and experience lessons with so that things could become unraveled and healed for the good of all involved. While none of this has ever felt lucky for me during the encounters of traumatic events, I have become able to switch my narratives and see things from a different perspective through healing the pain encoded within. Most of my traumas have not been mine at all but rather belong to my family, which I agreed to come here and help clean up. In my chapter of the *Own Your Awesome* book, I will tell you my story of discovering "Is this even mine?"

Some traumas become family secrets, leaving one to consume and store all the emotions inside. When one is not allowed to speak, it affects the throat chakra, causing thyroid issues. Everything then begins to build up with no way to get out, so it can start to spiral and manifest its way into something even more damaging. It may start to eat away at the immune system, wreaking havoc and causing autoimmune diseases and continuing to manifest as other diseases when one is still unaware of this trauma sitting there stored within the throat. All the fear, shame, guilt, and unlovable feelings become a true belief because that is what the brain believes and is allowed to come through as truth. Now becoming humiliated by these thoughts and disgusting feelings, she hides deep within, losing that light she once held. The judgments of others start to worry her, and feelings of the what-ifs become terrifying as there is no way to know what her perpetrator could do or even say if she were to speak up. Being engulfed in fear of what will happen if you speak out is very real and very scary. Hearing someone say that it's okay to speak out is not even enough trust to penetrate this field of mind absurdity. Deep down, she knew it was okay to speak out, but the fear stole her tongue and cursed her from speaking the truth. Years are spent smothered in feelings of terror. Outside, she struggles to maintain a composure that one might see as a happy, okay person. Pressure builds, and things continue to happen to her, but the fear is still holding her tongue from screaming or telling the truth. That one last touch from the darkness of this monster sends an explosion of anger and guilt into the chaos of her mind. It is now she gains enough energy to give up her fearful thoughts, not caring about the what-ifs or if he took her life for speaking out. All those scary feelings she was hanging onto for years built up and produced this tornado that was ready to unleash the truth.

It was as if she found a superpower of strength hidden within that helped guide her into the courageous, bold woman she was, allowing the curse to be ripped from her tongue. As she began to riddle the words off her tongue, it felt freeing, but it went south really quickly. The ones she told looked at her in disbelief that anything she was saying had occurred. Confused and left to fill back up with negative beliefs, the curse sneaks its way back to her tongue and shuts her down even further into the darkness. Now she is holding those heavy weights on her shoulders, and her heart is smothered in grief and shame, allowing her entire body to become a neurological mess. An inner ticking time bomb is now set and it feels like another puzzle must be unraveled in order to escape this curse and entrapment. Seeking the help of a psychiatrist, who labels her with a list of diseases and hands prescriptions her way as a means of helping her cope with the effects of the unfolding of traumatizing events in her life. In each session, she is asked questions and, based on her answers, determines the severity and level of dosage needed to simply help her numb the pain and help her sleep. Feeling guilty and ashamed every time she has to take the handful of pills, she swallows them down, numbing away the true pain.

"Hey, are you okay? Because you seem distant." A reminder that she is not functioning as a 'normal' human being rings loud through her thoughts. A quick response of "I'm fine" is uttered from her mouth with an embarrassing head turn as she is coping with social anxiety. The thoughts became loud in her mind. No one would understand her even if she told them. Thoughts like, 'No one cares what happens to you; they're just gonna call you a liar and say it is probably because of the way you dress.' She fully believes these thoughts that have consumed her beliefs and produced feelings that she is unlovable. The curse of the tongue is trying to take over her mind too! Fighting inside herself has become so exhausting, but she gathers what energy she can to keep up the fight on a daily basis. As thoughts began to set in, Crystal would question everything and build up anger towards those she once faced with her truth. Forgiveness shouts from the background, but in her mind, she cannot fathom the thought of forgiving those that have hurt her so. With some courage and lots of alcohol intake, she managed to face those again with the set intention of forgiving them but was unsuccessful with the forgiveness. Allowing them back into her life only opened that box down memory lane and reminded her of those traumatizing events. Desperate to feel loved, she attempted to stick to the forgiveness of others, but she was battling herself inside and covering it with alcoholism and a pack of cigarettes a day. Drinking had now become a sun up to sun down ritual to numb herself out. All the while missing the red flag in her current relationship with her partner. With him noticing she was spinning out of control with her drinking, it became apparent that he would need to talk to her about it. Crystal couldn't see drinking as a problem because she only saw it as a coping mechanism for making everything go away temporarily. It took her partner telling her that he was going to leave her when the reality slap hit her. At that moment, she realized this was not her, nor who she desired to be.

After a big detox and meltdown from the realization of her behavior, she began to awaken and, following a missed period with a positive pregnancy test, would rapidly shift this behavior. No more alcohol or cigarettes to cope with, and numb, knowing she had this little life to share her body with, she began cleaning herself up. This meant finding things to replace her coping methods of the usual drinking and smoking. So it began with learning how to make home-cooked meals from scratch, making crafts and enjoying a coffee when she had a desire for a drink. These new coping tools worked quite well as they kept her busy and away from the constant negative thinking. The pregnancy was defined as high risk around 16 weeks gestation, and a test result showed the potential of the new baby having spina bifida. This was very emotional for her to process as she had feelings and thoughts creeping in that it was her fault. Doctors recommended seeing a high-risk doctor from then on up until term to keep an eye on the new baby's growth and spinal area. Although things turned out alright, the new baby was ready to be born before term, which sent her into pre-labor. The doctor decided to go ahead and take him 5 ½ weeks early, meaning he would need extra care in the NICU. He was born and immediately had to be taken away from her and placed on oxygen due to his lungs not being fully developed yet. So, after an extra week in the hospital, they can go home, and now Crystal is busy non-stop. This new baby had come in and changed her entire life for the better.

The next big change was agreeing to leave her home state and move along with her partner for better work. Thoughts proceeded along in her head, and after some careful thinking, she decided to move. Nothing was holding her in place there anymore, and her oldest daughter's father had stopped all communication and attempts to visit. She was suffering from a miscarriage and recently lost her best friend along with her aunt in a car wreck. The grief was just eating at her, and it felt like it was time for something new in her life. Without hesitation, she agreed with her partner, and they began packing up to move seven hours away from her hometown. This was where the next set of challenges would lead her to a spiritual awakening, sending her to explore how to heal herself. With the offer on the table and the work promised, they arrived in the new town, which was beautiful. Things were so different than back home. The people were much nicer and drove slower, which was kinda annoying to adjust to, as back home, people drove really fast. Crystal and her partner crammed all their stuff into a garage and settled into a tiny apartment with their two kids. A few weeks after settling in, Crystal realizes she has missed her period and grabs a pregnancy test which says she is pregnant again. Scared to share the news, she waited 13 weeks this time to make an announcement. After the first 3 months in this new town, the work that was promised just wasn't available as promised. This led to seeking another opportunity farther out into another new town. Her youngest sister was willing to help and encouraged them to move upstate to live around her. She would send Crystal emails about jobs available in the area, but none were just right and her partner settled for one that was only two hours from the town they were currently in. This time they crammed their life into a rented trailer and made it home for a year. During this time, Crystal had given birth to a new baby daughter and was now super busy with a pre-teen, a 3-year-old that was becoming a runner and a newborn.

The baby is now almost four months old, and Crystal is up late one night, unable to sleep, tossing and turning. It is after 11 at night when her phone rings, and it shows Dad calling. Immediately her gut sank because she was hit intuitively with feelings that something was wrong. She answers the phone, and at the other end of the line, her dad says, "Crystal, I got some bad news; your sister is gone; she committed suicide." Suddenly, everything was blank feeling and processing was so slow that no words could fall out of her mouth. She began to blame herself for not moving there closer and being able to support her. Everything that came next was a blur of confusion spiraling around in her thoughts. From the crazy plane ride with two little ones to meeting her dad at the front door at 4 in the morning. This was supposed to be different. It was all she could think about. A visit here to see her sister was how it was supposed to be, but she was not there now, and she hated herself for it.

About a year later, they passed the medical cannabis law in Oklahoma, and Crystal felt guided towards it as a means to help her cope with pain and start to laugh again. With a doctor's appointment and approval, she was able to get a license. She was able to function with more ease and play with her three children while also improving her relationship with herself and her partner. Moving along, Crystal decided to try homeschooling her son, and that is when they discovered his brain worked differently and that she would need some extra help. Seeking out a therapist that could work with her, she found one that agreed to meet her at the library for a consultation. In that same week, she gets a call from her ex-husband's aunt, but she ignores it. Then the text messages began flowing in, and she was told to call her ex's father as soon as she could. The words fell out of his mouth, "He killed himself." She felt that familiar feeling when her gut sunk, and things went blank, searching for the right words to come out. This time she had to gather the strength to tell her daughter that her dad had passed away. Anxiously awaiting the therapy consultation, Crystal started crying while trying to tell the therapist what was going on, and at that moment, the therapist agreed to take on the whole family for therapy sessions. This was when the healing started to occur as therapy opened her box of trauma slowly, allowing her to pull forward and process things as needed. Through network marketing, self-help books, Facebook groups, and medical cannabis, she was guided into a spiritual awakening process. Grief, fear, and shame were the driving forces encouraging her to find herself that she lost back 10 years ago. Becoming aware of this new knowledge increased her drive to learn how to heal. Reading books is now becoming a favorite hobby of hers which she once hadn't any desire to do. By following mentors and learning how to say yes to herself, she found a healing modality that would steer her in the right direction to healing herself and learning how to help others heal.

Crystal is now fascinated with mind, body, and soul learning. How and why things work out the way they do is her new addiction. Through this growth, she's learned things about herself and things about why those who caused her pain did so. Finally, figuring out that forgiveness is a process we go thru, just like grief. There are stages of processing and no way to tell how long it will take to heal. Crystal learned what boundaries were and how to place them when others would try to overstep her, taking away her energy. Asking, "Truth is this even mine?" Bringing these things into her awareness gave her the opportunity to discern the thought, and then returning what was not hers back to the sender helped her gain some power back. That courageous soul that entered this planet from the beginning was climbing out of that tornado she had built within her mind, and no longer was she carrying the family curse. Making moves, she began setting intentions on her life path while gathering certificates in energy healing modalities, homeopathy, and one that she dedicated a few years of work to; a Certified D-codes practitioner. No one is more proud than she is of her accomplishments through life's traumatic events. She had held a sign that read "sink or swim," so she swam.

The abandonment, sexual trauma, divorce, miscarriage, loss of those to suicide, and car wrecks were all part of Crystal finding herself again and sparking her spiritual awakening. While this seems like an unfair process of life, something great happens. Where there is bad, there is also good. In the end, she likes to remind herself of this: it's not always going to be rainbows and butterflies. Because it takes a storm to create a rainbow, and the caterpillar must turn to goop before becoming a butterfly.

CHAPTER

Choose Happy, Not Crappy
By Mel Cassitta

Mel Cassitta is a Holistic Health and Happiness Specialist who transforms lives using her experience. After con-
quering esophageal cancer twice—and currently enduring liver failure—she infuses her resilience into helping
people achieve their best lives. Mel credits the surgeries,
chemotherapy, and radiation for saving her life, yet swears
her mind, body, and spiritual transformation was her best

medicine. Her journey became the catalyst for helping others, and sharing these gifts with those struggling has become her purpose.

Mel works with clients who seek positive support as they bridge the gap between where they are and where they would like to be. Her approach combines mindfulness, movement, and meditation to achieve balance while offering accountability to reach success. Mel coined the phrase "choose happy, not crappy" and has made it her mission to change as many mindsets as possible with her optimism and passion for life.

Mel's coaching program emphasizes that one's thoughts and beliefs are paramount to achieving happiness and healing. She continues to reap the benefits of her teachings and finds joy in spending time with her husband and children.

Reach Mel via email mel@melcassitta.com and Instagram @mels_army, or website melcassitta.com

Chapter 3

Choose Happy, Not Crappy

By Mel Cassitta

H I, I'M MEL CASSITTA, and the one thing that I want you to know about me is that choosing happiness saved my life. When I say it, I still think it sounds a bit dramatic. Then I take a moment and think about what the years since being diagnosed with esophageal cancer twice have entailed.

It all began in 2014 when I was 43 years old. I was and still am happily married to the love of my life. At the time, we had a 9-year-old daughter and a 16-year-old son. Today they are two of the most resilient people I know. My crazy cancer helped mold and shape them, proving that out of our darkest moments, beautiful lessons can be learned. My badass husband was a DEA Agent at the time and immediately jumped into the role of caregiver. His love and comfort were overwhelming and helped me survive. As for me, I was the Head Coach at an Orangetheory Fitness. Fitness was my passion. I worked 6 days a week and taught 18 classes. I was in excellent health but was having trouble with my voice. I had polyps on my vocal cords, and they burned so bad. When I couldn't get any relief, I went to a gastroenterologist to see if I had reflux. I had an endoscopy, and she said all looked awesome, but she'd have the results in a few days. I knew something was wrong because I was so uncomfortable, but I never imagined getting that dreaded phone call. The call that we all fear, the call that we all hope will never happen. I remember it like it was yesterday. I was at my daughter Isabella's school for a holiday party. I had the biggest smile as I was getting in the car to leave. It was a joy to be with her and all her classmates celebrating the holiday season. As I was getting in my car, I got a call from the Cleveland Clinic, and they asked if I could come in today; they had my endoscopy results. It sounded urgent and frightened me. I was in shock. I immediately called my husband, Rob, and asked him if he could come with me. The 10-minute drive felt like an hour, and we hardly said anything. We knew we were getting some bad news, but we never imagined being told I had Stage 0 esophageal cancer. Stage 0 means no chemotherapy and no radiation, but I would need an esophagectomy which is the surgical removal of the esophagus. They would remove my esophagus and pull up my stomach to replace it. The first thing I thought was, I've never heard of this. I've never ever seen this on *Grey's Anatomy*. After returning home, I was in the darkest place ever. I started to read about esophageal cancer, and the survival rate was not promising. I remember hiding in my bathroom, crying my eyes out, and seeing my life flash before my eyes.

I went to one of the top Surgical Oncologists at the University of Miami, and we set my surgery for February 3, 2014. He assured me that I'd be good to go once the cancer was removed. I trusted him and decided to put all my fear aside and make the best of it. I started to look at the situation logically. I was absolutely healthy. All we needed to do was remove the cancer, and I'd be 100% healthy. I'd have to recover from the surgery, which would be challenging, but I had a moment of true clarity. I thought someone had to be the best at recovering from this surgery, and that was going to be me. I started taking four Orangetheory classes weekly so I could be at my strongest. I also started going to the gym and lifting heavy weights. I was officially in training for my surgery. There was an inner voice telling me to be bold.

My clarity brought me focus, so I made a plan and reminded myself of it each and every day. I'd be the best at recovering so I could get back to life ASAP. On February 3, 2014, I went in for surgery. I was in ICU for three nights and then in the hospital for five.

It was fierce. They slit me open from my navel to my sternum. It felt like I would split open when I coughed, sneezed, or laughed. I was so happy to finally get home. I had peace of mind that the cancer was gone. All I needed was to recover, and then I could return to life. I made a ridiculous goal of getting back to teaching Orangetheory in six weeks. My goal was to work my way up to walking two miles. I'd always track my steps when I taught, so I knew that I generally walked two miles during each class. I was determined. I wanted to put this all behind me.

I started to take each day minute by minute. I walked daily, gained strength, and was back to work in six weeks. It felt amazing. I couldn't believe I did it. Everyone was impressed, inspired, and motivated, and it was terrific. I chose happy despite my awful, scary, unfair, and intensely crappy situation. But I never looked back and went all in and chose happy instead of allowing myself to feel crappy.

I had a lot of digestive issues. My new anatomy needed to settle in and everything needed to start working correctly. I struggled each day but accepted my new normal and made the best of each moment. It took about 8 months to begin feeling 75% better. I was still happy at that point, but I felt a bit lost. I had gone through this horrific experience, rushed back to life, but felt pretty empty.

I felt empty because I experienced a lot but didn't learn much. Something was missing. I was aware I had missed some messages and life lessons. I thought the big win was being healthy and getting back to life, but it was clear that was not the big win.

Two years later, I started to feel crappy. It was a nightmare. In December 2016, I started having horrific acid reflux episodes. It was one of the worst things I had ever experienced. They occurred around 2am, and I'd jump out of bed because I'd get a burning sensation going up through my ears and behind my eyes. I got with my gastroenterologist, we did tests, and everything looked great.

I had acid issues since my esophagectomy, so it seemed like this was a new side effect from surgery. Months went by, and the horrific acid episodes happened more and more. By April, I was so sick and had lost 15 pounds. I had a gastric emptying study, which showed that my stomach was not digesting food, and I was diagnosed with gastroparesis, paralysis of the stomach. At this point, I couldn't eat solid foods. I'd eat an egg and one piece of toast in the morning, and then it was nutritional shakes all day long. I'd drag myself out of bed and through my whole entire day. I figured this is life with gastroparesis, so get used to it. Again I told myself someone has to be the best at this.

By the time the weekend rolled around, I was too tired to talk. It was absolutely awful. I'll never forget one day I was on the couch in a complete daze. My husband was talking to me, and it was as if I couldn't comprehend what he was saying. I wanted to seem engaged, so I got up and walked to the kitchen counter near him. It took tremendous effort for me to take those 20 steps. I propped myself up against the counter, and suddenly I thought, this is what it must feel like to be dying. I was absolutely shocked. I couldn't believe that thought had occurred. Somehow, I made it through May, and then it was June. At this point, I lost 25 lbs. I was lighter than I was in high school. On June 21, I taught my 5am and 6am classes at Orangetheory and then went to Pure Barre for my 8am and 9am. You may wonder, how in the world did I get through this? It was the energy. I always felt a fantastic vibe while teaching. Everyone in the room was motivated and had a goal. It always took my mind to another place. That is what happens when you surround yourself with positivity.

Afterward, I went home to take a nap. I sat on the couch and propped up pillows next to me so I could lean into them. Within five minutes, the acid happened. I freaked out and called my doctor. She told me to go to the emergency room.

My daughter was sleeping, so I woke her up and told her I was fine, but I was going to drive myself to the emergency room. That was not a good moment, but I needed relief. I needed comfort. I needed help. I couldn't believe I had to leave my little girl in such a worried state. She was only 13, and she looked so concerned and scared. It was one of the most awful moments of my life.

I was so relieved to be in the hospital. I loved laying in the hospital bed. I loved having an IV and that they were going to take tests. The first thing they were going to do was a scan. The technician was so caring. I told him my symptoms, and he looked a bit concerned. He took the scan, and I could see his extreme sympathy as soon as he read it. You know how you always imagine your doctor or technician looking at you like something is wrong. This time there was absolutely no mistaking the fact that there was something horribly wrong. He even put his hand on my shoulder and wished me the best. I had an 'oh shit' moment. My gastroenterologist looked at the scan and was in shock. She couldn't quite get the words out. Finally, she said, you have a 12-centimeter tumor attached to the outside of your stomach. It was not seen during the endoscopy because it was attached to the outside of the stomach.

She immediately assured me it might be a bleed and not a tumor. At this point, I didn't even care if it was a tumor. I actually felt relieved. It was all starting to make sense. I couldn't eat because there was a tumor the size of a softball attached to my stomach. I was admitted to the hospital, and over the next seven days, we would figure out precisely what this was. I was diagnosed with metastatic cancer to the retroperitoneum. The cancer had returned as a 12-centimeter tumor attached to the outside of my stomach. I had spots on my liver and activity in my gallbladder. The tumor was so large that it was pressing on my lungs, displaced my liver, and was near my aorta. There was no way the cancer could be removed, so I needed radiation and chemotherapy. They told my husband the focus was to get me through a year. Unfortunately, they predicted a poor outcome. My husband kept this to himself and never told me. I believe this was a crucial component in my recovery. As they say, what you don't know won't hurt you. I had dark days. I was afraid, frail, and sick. They put a pic line in my arm, and I started to get lots of nutrition. Once again, my clarity kicked in. I began to shift my mindset to what was going well. My body was receiving nutrients. This allowed me to get stronger, making me feel better physically and mentally. This was going to be a long road, and being depressed and in a dark place would only make my battle more challenging. I started to read devotionals and anything I could find that was inspiring and peaceful.

I was grateful for everything my husband, kids, family, and friends had done for me. Every single person that worked at the hospital was amazing. The support and love that my family and friends gave me daily were so comforting. I had an NG tube up my nose, which went down into my stomach. It was constant discomfort. The pain that the tumor created was intense. The tumor was so large that I constantly had a fever. It was sucking the life out of me. I had crappy moments, but I continuously reminded myself to choose happy and enjoy each day second by second.

I left the hospital and started chemotherapy a few days later, and things got dark quick. It all felt extremely crappy. A million questions came to mind. Are my doctors the right doctors? Is there a better treatment plan? Should I be in a trial? Is this the right chemo? I had a complete mental breakdown, and one of my doctors walked into the room. I cried, and she looked at me and said, "You are in the right place and getting the best treatment." She promised me that if this course of treatment did not get me results, she would help me find another treatment method. I was very open, and this allowed me to have trust in her and be hopeful.

At that moment, I chose to believe and felt such a tremendous sense of peace. I had the full belief that I was on the right path. I never once questioned my treatment and didn't search for other doctors. I did not go on blogs to hear about other people's experiences. I could barely handle my experience. The last thing I needed was to be consumed by others. One of the most crucial things for us all to understand is that our minds do not know the difference between what's happening to us or someone else. When we start thinking, our brain turns on switches, and our whole body becomes affected. For example, say I read many blogs on esophageal cancer, and everyone is suffering, hates their doctors, and questions their treatment. I would feel concerned, worried, fearful, tense, and stressed. Meanwhile, these are someone else's experiences. They are not happening to me. I reminded myself that in the present moment, I was sitting in my peaceful home lounging on the couch with my husband and kids, and as they were watching a funny show, I was reading and living someone else's nightmare blog. Every time I read, I became hopeless, depressed, and anxious. From the second I started researching my cancer and diagnosis, my intuition told me to stop, but I couldn't.

Something reminded me that I had the choice to be happy. All I had to do was have belief. From that point, I cast aside fear, worry, and doubt. I dove into mindfulness, yoga, meditation, essential oils, tapping, and reading daily devotionals. I became a reiki student, learned all I could about energy healing, and became a reiki master. I enrolled in a 6-week happiness course. I focused on believing in recovery, love, patience, kindness, and joy. It made my spirit come alive. When you feel good, your body creates happiness hormones that relax, calm, block pain, and make you more social. This brought me to a place of peace, and I could feel that happiness was starting to save me.

I was choosing happy and feeling at peace. I started to have a clear vision of recovering and being healthy again. I knew I could die, but I never once imagined myself dying. How sick I felt, how debilitated my body was, and how fearful I was of my treatment all became secondary thoughts. Something told me to put those fearful thoughts to the side, and every time I did, I felt as if I was being healed. My daily focus is to be at peace, find happiness, and spread love. This makes me feel whole because even when I was deathly ill, in my mind, I honestly was in a beautiful place. Right from the beginning, it was evident to me that negative thoughts were the disease that would kill me. I had no control over my cancer, but I had total control of my thoughts. I decided if my time was going to be limited, I wanted each moment to bring me joy. To make that happen, I knew I needed to cast aside crappy and bring in happy.

I ended my cancer treatment on October 16, 2017, and have been entirely cancer-free. I am now in liver failure and will need a liver transplant. This is due to the excessive radiation that was necessary to get rid of the massive tumor I had. Mentally and physically, dealing with liver failure is a daily battle, but thankfully I am mastering choosing happy, not crappy.

Here's the big message I bring to you. Learning to choose happy, not crappy, was the big epiphany that came to me when I was dying. I believe that my first cancer wasn't a big enough lesson so cancer came again. In that near-death experience, the vast message that came through loud and clear was that we always have a choice. Choice is our superpower. Our choices can always bring us to a better place. I am so thankful to have received this message and grateful to share it with all of you. It has brought comfort to many, and I will continue my mission of spreading this message so that we can all live a life in comfort and peace.

CHAPTER

How This Introvert
Operates Boldly
By Pamela Duncan

Pam points to her 5th-grade report on Gandhi and then a book on past life regression as the beginning of her awareness of a spiritual journey and knowing that there was more to this life than what we see on the surface.

While raising a son and a daughter, she volunteered, worked as an office manager, and completed a Bachelor's

Degree. Just as Pam was about to become an empty nester, a tragedy thrust her into a more profound spiritual awakening and created a path she had never envisioned. She discovered her strength and resilience.

In addition, over the next two decades, health challenges, including Lyme Disease and toxic mold exposure, led her to become an Institute for Integrative Nutrition Holistic Health Coach and later a Clinical Hypnotherapy Practitioner and Integrative Life Coach through the Schaefer Institute of Hypnosis.

Pam's passion is in helping others who have experienced loss and health issues. Performing random acts of kindness brings her joy, and she is a believer in miracles! Pam can be reached at pmd.aloha@gmail.com.

Chapter 4

How This Introvert Operates Boldly

By Pamela Duncan

P OSSESSING A MORE INTROVERTED personality, I had to give serious thought to the offer of adding a chapter to a book titled, *Be Bold*. I spent time mining my history for evidence of bold behavior. What I found was a thread that weaves through four decades. Pivotal moments of going against the tide that did not necessarily feel bold at the time but in retrospect, all had become essential steps leading to bold actions in the toughest, darkest days of my life. The backdrop for these most fearless actions? A church and a courtroom.

There may be no way of knowing if we are born with a personality type or if our environment shapes us as much or more than our genetic makeup. Was I born quiet and shy, or more likely, did an unpredictable environment infused with alcoholism frighten the outgoing girl right out of me? I remember feeling much safer when I was quiet and unnoticed. So, I did my best to behave and blend into the wallpaper.

Doesn't the entire world prefer us all to be as extroverted and outgoing as Tony Robbins, Oprah, or the menagerie of politicians we face daily? Aren't we all thinking that in order to be successful, we must be as loud, public, and competitive as the aggressive personalities that demand our attention as soon as we turn on a screen?

In her book, *Quiet*, Susan Cain explains that when most of the population lived on farms and in small communities for an entire lifetime being introverted or extroverted was not the significant divide it is today. With the onset of the Industrial Revolution and the mass migration to the cities came the need for people to express more personality. A person's character became overridden by the need to be able to *sell* themselves. Cain sees this as the era when introverts began to exist at a disadvantage. With the advent of television and social media, the shy and quiet have faded into the background even more. You may have brilliant ideas, but you must stand up and sell them to an audience to succeed in these times.

I felt the disadvantage that Susan Cain writes about in *Quiet*. I felt it whenever I was labeled shy and would often beat myself up for it. When my father's job change forced us to move to a new town and a new school, I was entering eighth grade. I entered as my shy, introverted self, hoping to blend in. It didn't take long for me to start hearing rumors that I was labeled "stuck up." Being misunderstood in that way forced me to step beyond my comfort zone and do my best to be more outgoing and involved. *Fake it until you make it* became my motto. When my parents divorced and moving again for my senior year of high school became necessary, I knew the drill. I did fit in more quickly this time but never was comfortable going against my quiet nature.

I was, for the most part, a good student. I liked the predictability of school and was happy to follow the rules. A challenger I was not. At home, I loved my desk, and the responsibility of homework allowed me to be alone in my bedroom with fewer interruptions. If my father was home, my two younger sisters and I had to look as though we were being productive; no watching TV and no sitting around were allowed. His motto was, *Get up. Get dressed. Get going!* On the other hand, our mom usually insisted that we be outside and not underfoot. All this attracted me to reading as an escape while I felt out of the way in my room.

One book had a considerable impact on me. When my fifth-grade teacher's assignment was to write a book report on a biography, I went to the school library and scanned shelves. With no one famous in mind, I looked at plenty of book covers until one struck me. The man's face was so warm and friendly. He was smiling, and I wanted to know more; he was not like anyone in the life I knew. The title was *Gandhi*, and the back cover explained his life as a lawyer and how his actions of peaceful resistance had freed a nation. That someone could be that influential without aggression filled me with a deep curiosity. What started as a book report would lead to a lifetime of inspiration down a path quite different from those around me.

During my formative years, many news stories were about the Vietnam War. At the same time, there were rumblings of a women's liberation movement. Women were protesting and wanted more than to stay home with children; they wanted careers. When so often asked what I wanted to be when I grew up, I felt embarrassed to say that I wanted to have children and raise them. In those days, it was bold to go against the tide of Women's Lib; I felt like a traitor to my entire gender! As a child, playing teacher with my sisters as my students had been fun, but I did not think I wanted a career, at least not right away. I wanted to have children, teach *them* and be home when they were young. My deepest desire was to create the family I wished I had had growing up.

Going to college was expected, so I went through the motions. I began at a school within driving distance; my parents had divorced, and my mom was getting married again. It was a tumultuous time. Looking back on it now, I felt I needed to be present for my younger sisters. During freshman year, I was inspired by classes in physical geography. I had always been fascinated with maps and loved the graphics classes I had taken in high school. My professor informed me that a university about an hour away offered a major in cartography. He thought that I would excel in that field and even offered to take me there for a visit. That offer raised my confidence level more than he could have known.

After the campus visit, I was genuinely grateful to my professor and motivated to plan to attend the next school year. I excitedly approached my mom with the idea that I would eventually transfer there, and she discouragingly said, "What are you going to do with that?" I had no idea; I just wanted to do something I was interested in until I could fulfill my dream of having my own family. It didn't take long after that for me to lose interest in college and make one of my first bold decisions—to quit. I had rarely gone against my family's expectations, and this was a big step in paving my path.

"It takes a fair amount of boldness and courage to step out of those normal constrictions and very narrow ways of perceiving." —Sharon Salzberg, author and meditation teacher

Influenced by my desire to get on with adult life and a diagnosis of endometriosis, which could render me infertile, I married at the age of 20. My sisters, off to college hours away, gave me the feeling of permission to go where the future would lead us. Now a Navy wife, there were many moves ahead as we began our new life almost two thousand miles from home.

I gave birth to our daughter at one Naval assignment and, fifteen months later, a son at our following location. Both brought great feelings of love and accomplishment; I was incredibly proud. They were beautiful and perfect in my eyes. I was on my way to creating my dream family. I had withstood the peer pressure of career-minded women. While I adored being home with my children, it was tremendously challenging to be raising them so alone, so geographically far from family. I had not pictured this part, being so alone, isolated, and sleep-deprived! I had not been a part of the decision to become a military family. In those days, there were long deployments, little support, no babysitters, and no internet. I was even told by my husband not to make a long-distance phone call; we couldn't afford it. My only way of communicating with friends and family was by writing letters and hoping they would write back or, even better, call me. The show *Cheers* was on Thursday nights in those days. I would turn it on and cry with the lyrics of the song:

"...Sometimes you want to go

Where everybody knows your name

And they're always glad you came

You want to be where you can see

Our troubles are all the same

You want to be where everybody knows your name...."

With two children to nurture and raise, I played my role and did a tremendous amount of research on parenting. I wanted a calmer, more proactive parenting style than I had experienced. I took the gift of these two souls very seriously and wanted to be the best possible mom for them. I wanted them to know I would be there doing my best to nurture and support them, cheering them on, believing in them, advocating boldly and firmly for them when needed, and comforting them if things didn't go as planned.

After more than a decade of giving, I felt depleted, lonely, and lost. Who was I now? I didn't feel appreciated or loved; I felt taken for granted, unseen, and unheard. I was playing the role of the good wife, mom, and daughter, doing what was expected with a smile, accepting crumbs, and not being bold on my own behalf. I had communicated my feelings and come up against a stone wall time after time. So similar to my childhood experience, one cannot have a better relationship with another who avoids participating. I needed to find my way forward, and after living through my parent's divorce, in my mid-teens, I did not feel that that was the best route for us at the time. I wanted to spare my children the ugliness of divorce and create happy childhood memories. I also wanted to inspire them to go on to college while at the same time preparing myself for the many options that lay ahead.

Standing in line at a Boy Scout event, I said to my best friend, "I want to go back to college."

She said, "I do too. I would do that with you." I was well into my thirties, and this would be a bold move! I'd be going back into the classroom twice a week with students half my age in addition to raising a family, taking care of our home, and working 30 hours per week. Grateful that she wanted to go along for the ride, feeling energized, excited, and financially backed by people other than myself and my husband, I enrolled against his wishes.

I found college to be challenging and validating. I still enjoyed school and pushing myself to get good grades. After completing many of the required courses, I had time to explore electives. I tried music history and a film class, but the legal courses drew me in time after time. I gravitated to those offerings so much that when I graduated, I went and spoke to one of the law professors about continuing to law school. He listened to my interest and said, "You don't want to do that; it's a nasty business." That was the end of that; I put the idea aside.

Our daughter would be off to college in a few months, and I decided to push my endeavors off until after our son's high school graduation and his transition to college in another year. Being free to enjoy his senior year and go to his games, along with visiting my daughter at college, would be the best way to wind down this phase of my life.

We were devastated as a Higher Power had another direction in mind. Our son's life was taken in an auto vs. truck accident. He was leaving his part-time job, doing one errand, and coming home for dinner on a winter night. Suddenly everything was different; all priorities turned upside down and shaken to the core. How? Why? Saying our lives would never be the same was an understatement. So much love and kindness had been taken from the planet along with his joyful soul.

Our home filled quickly with grieving friends and family who did not want to be alone. We gathered, shared our shock, cried, and told stories of his kindness, generous spirit, and infectious smile. At a time when I could have curled up and refused to leave my bed, I instead became uplifted by what I felt was a communication, or a sign, from my son that came exactly 12 hours after the accident.

Because I had had this interaction, I knew without a doubt that his spirit still existed somewhere and that we would still be able to communicate. I became the leader by default. I planned the service with the help of girlfriends, and I would give his eulogy. I was bold in a way I never knew was possible.

Days became weeks, and we still did not know what happened during the accident. The police report took much longer than people with a knowledge greater than ours had expected. I found solace in the beautiful letters arriving, telling stories of our son's generosity, good deeds, and random acts of kindness. Finally, the report was ready. However, it gave us few answers and no comfort; how could *neither* party be at fault? Our son was dead, and the other young man, the truck driver, had refused medical care and gone home to sleep in his own bed that night. We were then even more confused, which weighed heavily on the fog of grief that continued to swirl in our heads.

Some had suggested we file a lawsuit. I considered that advice, researched, made a few calls, and then remembered my law professor saying, "You don't want to do that; it's a nasty business." I quickly concluded that no legal action would be the right avenue. I needed my energy for healing, helping our family, especially our daughter, now back at college, and moving us all forward. No legal outcome would bring our son back.

Almost two years after the accident, the phone rang in early January. I'll never forget the woman's sad, apologizing tone as she explained that she was from our insurance company and my husband was being sued as the legal owner of the car our son had been driving. There would be papers arriving later that day, drawing us into a lawsuit filed by the truck driver. His basis? PTSD. He claimed to have posttraumatic stress from the accident in which our son had lost his life, and money from us was his solution. He wanted more money than the insurance company was willing to give him. What kind of insanity is this? I was in disbelief! The woman must've said, "I'm so sorry," at least two dozen times.

I spent about half an hour feeling out of control and not knowing which direction to go. Then something came over me, and I thought, if this is coming at us, *it is a gift*. I will win this. The fierce but calm mama lion in me emerged.

As part of our healing process, we occasionally found comfort across the table from an intuitive woman with some gifts in mediumship. A good friend introduced us to her shortly after the accident. We had an appointment the same day the insurance phone call came in. Amazingly, she had canceled our meeting before Christmas and rescheduled it for this same day. I would ask her for advice. Perfect timing or, as I prefer, great synchronicity!

Amazingly, she had a friend who worked for a very experienced trial lawyer educated at both Harvard and Yale. I made an appointment to see him. After two weeks of research and consideration, he agreed to help us. I would be countersuing. Assisting him in the process was grueling. After all, he did not know my son, and I had to endure the painful process of educating him about the unique soul whose life was taken. I had hoped for an out-of-court settlement to end this quickly. However, no offer came. I made myself available to help in any way I could. The trial was first scheduled for fall, then spring, then fall, and on and on for three and a half years before a date stuck.

Jury selection began on my birthday, another sign that kept me believing this would be a gift. We participated in helping to select the jury, and I mentally sent them thoughts of gratitude every day. We sat in a courtroom for eleven weeks with five or more lawyers. Often the other driver was there. I drew on every skill I had, from yoga, meditation, and intuition, to listening intently, being hyper-aware of my surroundings, and never letting the other side hear me speak until I took the stand. I thought of Gandhi. Silence also has power.

The jury deliberated for two days when my lawyer seemed to lose faith in the case and started advising me to take a small, undetermined settlement. I had lived and breathed this case for four years. I had seen sign after sign that indicated I would win. I decided to stand my ground by boldly going against the advice of highly educated lawyers and my family. Firmly, I faced them with my decision and won!

A bittersweet win. We felt joy, and seconds later, we cried over the loss of such a rare human being. Round and round we went on that emotional ride. Again, our lives had been turned upside down.

CHAPTER

Five

Taking the Stage
By Karen Gabler

Karen Gabler is an award-winning attorney, intuitive mentor, psychic medium, animal communicator and Reiki master. She also is a best-selling author, teacher and inspirational speaker. Karen is passionate about encouraging others to find their highest purpose and live their best lives. She mentors her clients through a variety of personal and business issues, marrying her practical legal and business experience with her intuitive ability to receive information and guidance from higher sources. She also facilitates connections with clients' loved ones in spirit. Karen conducts workshops and presentations on a variety of business, spiritual and personal development topics. She earned her Bachelor of Science in psychology from the University of Hawaii and her Juris Doctorate from the William S. Richardson School of Law at the University of Hawaii. Karen has pursued wide-ranging education in interpersonal development and the spiritual sciences, working with tutors from the prestigious Arthur Findlay College for the Psychic Sciences in England as well as with numerous intuitives and mediums throughout the United States. She is a WCIT in the Martha Beck Wayfinder life coaching program. Karen enjoys reading, hiking, horseback riding and spending time with her husband and children. You can find Karen at www.karengabler.com.

Chapter 5

Taking the Stage

By Karen Gabler

I WAS LOUNGING IN bed on a rainy Saturday in 2004, scrolling through television channels to escape my boredom. A young man named John stood on a stage in front of a rapt audience, most of whom carried shocked expressions. He pointed to a gentleman seated with his arms crossed, frowning and skeptical. "Your son says that you carry a coin for him in your pocket." The gentleman gasped and reached into his pocket, pulling out a shiny coin. He looked up at John with watery eyes and said, "How did you know that?"

In the early 2000s, psychic medium John Edward hit the airwaves with his popular television show, *Crossing Over*. He made connections to people in spirit for his audience members, bringing through stunning evidence that their loved ones were still present, remaining close and sharing their lives after they passed on. Having lost my own parents at a young age, I was mesmerized by the idea that they might be able to communicate with me from beyond.

I was blown away by the evidence John was able to convey to his audience. I wondered if it would be possible to receive a private reading with him, but his website indicated that his waiting list was several years long and had been closed. As with most celebrities, he seemed out of reach in his television studio. I accepted that my experience with mediumship would have to be limited to catching John's television show and reassured myself that if other people's loved ones could show up to communicate with them, my loved ones must be near me as well.

As I had never heard of mediumship before, I assumed that this incredible skill must be unique to this one man – or perhaps just a small handful of special people in the world. When John scheduled a public demonstration of mediumship some years later, I joined several hundred people in a hotel ballroom to see him in person. I was surprised when he personally welcomed a few audience members, announcing that they were "fellow mediums." At the end of the program, he introduced a woman named Hollister Rand to the audience, noting that she was a terrific medium based in Hollywood – only 40 minutes away from me! As the crowd dispersed, I ran over to Hollister and asked for her contact information to schedule a reading with her.

A few short weeks later, I was perched on the couch in Hollister's office, listening in stunned silence as she connected with my deceased parents. She brought up a variety of information, all of which was true. As a born skeptic, though, I wasn't quite convinced. I wanted to believe, but my years of training as an attorney prompted me to search for clear evidence that she really was communicating with spirit. I wondered whether she had researched information about me before I came in, as I questioned whether she was truly talking to my parents.

I spoke to my mother in my own mind. "Mom, if this is really you, please tell her something that will prove to me that you're here." Despite my plea, my skepticism was enhanced when Hollister told me that my mother in spirit was talking about the "family party" we would be having in Chicago at my father's home that summer. I said, "There's no family party, and we're not going to Chicago this summer, so that's not right." She said, "Well, I don't know what to tell you, but your mother says that everyone is going to Chicago for a family party this summer."

Hollister wrapped up the session shortly thereafter, and I called my sister on the way home to tell her about the reading. "Well, she said a lot of things that were true, but she also said that Mom says we're going to a family party in Chicago this summer. That's clearly not right, so I just don't know about this." My sister drew a swift intake of breath and said, "You're not going to believe this...I just talked to Dad before you called. He says he's planning a family reunion party in Chicago this summer and wants us all to be there."

Several years later, I received a mailing list invitation to Hollister's upcoming workshop on connecting with spirit. I emailed her to announce that I was not a medium and certainly wasn't claiming to be one. I said I didn't want to disrupt her workshop, but just wanted to see if there was a way to feel my own parents around me more often, without getting a reading. She said, "Why don't you just come and see what happens?" I had no idea what to expect, but felt compelled to attend and decided to take the leap.

At the workshop, Hollister encouraged us to be relaxed and just experiment, have fun and be open. I was surprised to learn that the class was made up of over 40 professional and aspiring mediums. In our first exercise, I was paired with a lovely woman named Kim. With Hollister's guidance, Kim connected with my late grandmother and began to share information she couldn't possibly have known: the jewelry she wore, her wedding to my grandfather, the period of time when she cared for me as a baby.

When it was my turn, I looked up at Hollister, panic-stricken at the idea of having to connect with someone in spirit. She encouraged me to just say whatever popped into my mind, without any pressure to be right. I closed my eyes and began feeling as though I was in a daydream. I said, "Okay, I'm seeing a man, and he feels older, like a grandfather. He likes to play checkers...or maybe chess? He is sitting at a stone table in a park." I opened my eyes and Kim said, "Yes, that's my grandfather. He always liked to sit at this little stone table at the park and play chess with his best friend."

I was astonished that I had come up with information Kim could validate. Tears sprang to my eyes as I considered the significance of what had just happened. We were talking to people in spirit...*I was talking to people in spirit*...how was this possible? How did I do that? Could I really be a *medium*? Really? *Me*? I left the workshop floating on a cloud, and couldn't wait for the next opportunity to try it again.

I began studying with a variety of professional mediums in the United States as well as abroad, exploring the process of connecting with people in a spiritual dimension. I learned how to silence my brain's distracting thoughts, find the stillness within me, feel the presence of spirit around me, and interpret the information and messages that came through. It was like spiritual charades, and I quickly discovered that my logical brain – always so helpful in my legal work – was far less productive in spiritual work. I would feel a sense of a woman sitting in an armchair and my brain would promptly supply an image of the armchair found in my own living room to "help" me understand what I was feeling:

I can sense a woman sitting in a chair in the living room. She loves this chair. "She had a special chair she liked to sit in when she was in your living room?" I said to my sitter.

"Yes, she did! She sat in that chair every night!"

"The chair is brown leather?" I said hopefully.

"No, it's not brown, and it is not leather."

Hmmm...but I see brown leather, just like mine...oh, wait a minute...that's MY chair.

As time passed, I became more adept at distinguishing between my own thoughts or memories and the information that spirit was trying to share with me. I began to discern the true source of emotions bubbling up inside me. For a while, I would burst into tears whenever I felt the rush of love from spirit flooding my body as they rejoiced in being able to reach their loved ones. In my workshops and practice sessions, I received messages of love and encouragement through my classmates as they gave me readings, and I shared similar messages with them from their loved ones in spirit. The opportunity to experience repeated spirit connections was an astounding gift, and I was so grateful for the time I spent practicing with my fellow students.

Over time, my classmates began to take the lessons we had learned and share them with real clients, outside of the practice arena. They put up websites and posted on social media, connecting with the public and offering their mediumship services. I cheered them on, reminding them at every turn that they were doing incredible work. They would return the compliments and urge me to do the same. "When are you going to get out there? You're a fantastic medium, it's time for you to share it with others!" As much as I loved being able to give readings to my fellow students, something held me back from publicly announcing myself as a medium. When people asked me what I did, I responded simply that I was an attorney. I was reluctant to share my mediumship, thinking no one would believe that I could do something so incredible.

Despite my reluctance to "go public," I couldn't deny the healing opportunities that mediumship brought to the world. Those grieving the loss of their loved ones were able to reconnect, discovering that their deceased friends and family members continued to share their lives, celebrate their successes and support them in their challenges. People in spirit connected through me to thank their loved ones for taking care of them at the end of their human lives, or to let them know that they were aware of an upcoming birthday or a new baby in the family. It was apparent time and time again that mediumship work brought incredible love and healing. I wanted to give as many people as possible this amazing opportunity, but I still couldn't bring myself to advertise my abilities. I continued to hide, working only with my classmates within the safety of the classroom.

As my development progressed, I joined a year-long mediumship progressive group. The classes focused on mediumship demonstrations, much like the work I had seen John Edward do on television years before. The culmination of the class was to do a public demonstration, where we could take turns demonstrating mediumship to the public. I agreed to take the course, but assured my teacher and classmates that I had no intention of participating in the public demonstration. I promised to offer my unwavering support for their efforts, but insisted that I just wanted to enhance my mediumship, not present it on a stage.

Over the year, I remained resolute in my decision to skip the public event, as I was still unsure of my developing abilities. As the class neared its conclusion at the end of the year and plans for the public demonstration were underway, my classmates urged me once again to step out of my comfort zone and participate in the event with them. I continued to resist, even though I stood up in front of them over and over again, endlessly practicing my mediumship demonstration skills. On our last day of class, our teacher was bringing the session to a close and discussing the final schedule for that evening's presentation. He began to list the students in order of appearance. As he read the list of names, he looked at me and said, "Karen, it's time for you to demonstrate as well. You can do it. Let's put you third on the list."

My mouth dropped open as my classmates cheered. I began to protest, but in the face of their support and coming off of a week of successful class practice, I finally agreed to participate. It would be only ten minutes on stage...really, how bad could it be? I told myself I was ready for this; I had been in classes for years and had made hundreds of connections with the spirit world. I had laughed, cried and participated in profound healing experiences with my classmates. My teacher was right...I was ready!

We took a short break to relax and prepare ourselves for the evening, some of us quietly meditating and others chatting and laughing together. The excitement was palpable; we were going to give our first public demonstration together! As we returned to the hotel ballroom, however, utter panic suddenly washed over me, stopping me short. *What am I doing? What was I thinking? Why did I agree to do this? I can't do this! I'm not a medium! I'm a lawyer, for Pete's sake! I'm not ready for this! Who am I to think that I can stand up in front of a bunch of people and claim that I can talk to people in spirit? Who am I to act like I'm someone special?*

Like so many women of my generation, I was raised to be humble and to avoid bragging. I learned from an early age that we mustn't behave as though we think we are better than others, and it isn't polite to openly announce our skills and abilities to the world. As a child, I learned that "children should be seen and not heard." As a woman, I learned that being bold and standing out was cause for derision, rather than celebration. As a result, I attributed my successes to external factors. When I graduated with honors and passed the bar exam to become an attorney, I expressed gratitude for my teachers and the bar study program. When I won awards for my professional achievements, I credited my public relations team for their solid marketing efforts.

My mediumship was different, though. My mediumship classes could help me to improve my spirit communication skills, but I couldn't study or market my way into effective spirit connections. For the first time, I had to accept that this intuitive ability came from a place deep within my soul. It depended upon trusting myself and surrendering to the communication. And yet, the prospect of publicly expressing something remarkable about myself struck fear into my heart. I was so awed by the concept of spirit com-munication that I still couldn't fathom telling others that I was able to do it myself.

Author Marianne Williamson said, "Our deepest fear is not that we are inadequate. Our deepest fear is that we are powerful beyond measure. It is our light, not our darkness, that most frightens us. We ask ourselves, 'Who am I to be brilliant, gorgeous, talented, fabulous?' Actually who are you not to be? You are a child of God. Your playing small does not serve the world." The purpose of shining our light is to celebrate the gifts we've been given, and share those gifts with others. We honor our unique nature by rising up and bringing our best selves forward, which allows others to do the same. When we all shine, the world is filled with light.

As I took deep breaths in the lobby outside the hotel ballroom, trying to quell the anxiety rising within me, I suddenly realized that the act of announcing myself publicly as a medium wasn't selfish or self-important. Rather, focusing solely on my fear stripped away my joy, and made me reluctant to serve others in a way I was meant to serve. I have the ability to connect with people in spirit, to bring them closer to those who miss them here on earth. I have the ability to bring healing to others, in the spirit world as well as in the physical realm. People were attending this event in the hopes of hearing from someone they loved, and I was having a panic attack over whether I was willing to help them do so, instead of being deeply grateful that I *could* do so. I realized that the question I needed to ask myself was not "who am I to do this," but instead, "who am I *not* to do this?"

I straightened my shoulders and smiled as I walked onto the stage. I closed my eyes briefly, and felt a man and woman approach me from the spirit world. Grandfather and grandmother, holding hands in spirit just as they did in life. They smiled widely, and I felt the rush of love and joy they brought through me. I looked out at the sea of faces and said, "I have a grandfather and grandmother here with me, looking for their granddaughter. They were like two peas in a pod, always holding hands, always together. They loved to dance together, and their love for each other never wavered." A young lady in the front row gasped and her hand shot into the air. Tears filled her eyes as I shared stories of the special dishes her grandmother made for the holidays, and the dance recitals they watched in years gone by as their young granddaughter, now an adult in my audience, had twirled on stage. She wiped her eyes and clutched her friend's hand; her friend smiled at me and said to her, "I know how badly you wanted to hear from them; I'm so happy for you!"

I shared with the young lady that her grandparents had truly loved watching her dance on stage as a little girl, because it brought them so much joy to see her shine her light. I reminded her that they wanted her to continue shining her light in the world, and to know in her heart that they would dance along with her as she did so. As I brought the reading to a close, I silently thanked her grandparents for working with me, and then smiled as I promised myself that I would keep shining my own light and bringing joy to others as well.

CHAPTER

Six

The Ripple Effect
By Sarah Gabler

Sarah Gabler is 16 years old and in eleventh grade. She loves playing games with her family and traveling to new places. Sarah enjoys playing the ukulele and guitar, singing and dancing, and riding her horse. As a lifelong artist, she is pursuing graphic design and loves using creative outlets to express her artistic vision. She is a technical sound engineer for her high school productions and loves bringing a show to life to entertain others. She is passionate about empowering people by helping them to recognize their true potential in the world and plans to do motivational speaking in the future. Sarah began exploring spiritual

teachings, self-development and soul empowerment concepts when she was 10 years old and believes it has made
her a better person today. It has motivated her to find ways
to live her best life and to help others on their journey to
live their best lives as well. Sarah believes that even the
smallest act of kindness can make someone's day, and she
enjoys going out of her way to make others feel loved.

Chapter 6

The Ripple Effect

By Sarah Gabler

"*NEVER UNDERESTIMATE THE EMPOWERED empath. Our kindness and compassion is too often mistaken for weakness or naivety, while we are in fact highly calibrated human lie detectors and fearless warriors for truth and justice.*" —Anthon St. Maarten

I have always been an empath, sensitive to the energy and experiences of others. I am aware of how others are feeling, and highly focused on those who need help. Because I am more sensitive, I am prone to feeling overwhelmed with emotions that may not even be mine. I'm aware of this tendency, and have learned a lot about how to protect my energy.

Nevertheless, it wasn't until I stood up for a fellow student in my school that I learned about what it really means to be an empath. In the process of taking a stand on behalf of another person, I realized how powerful empathy can be. After a challenging situation, I had to be strong for myself as well as for others, and it created a ripple effect on those around me.

I have always been excited to walk onto campus at the beginning of every school year. New year, a new opportunity to be the greatest I can be! All the mistakes made in the previous year would be behind me and I would move forward, having learned from those experiences. I also crave new teachers, new subjects and new learning styles. I have never enjoyed repetition, and I need something different after following the same routines for an entire school year.

As I entered the gates of my middle school to begin seventh grade, I noticed that everyone seemed to have the same positive energy about the new school term (or so I thought). It was the start of a new year, and I was sure that it would be a positive and uplifting environment. I looked forward to making new friends and memories.

I walked into my new science class and saw a seating chart displayed on the whiteboard. As I searched for my name, I felt momentarily disheartened as I realized that I didn't know anyone in my class. I had been less of a talker and more of a "people watcher" in middle school, so most students in the school didn't have a clue who I was, even if I could easily pick them out of a crowd.

I finally found my name on the chart, seated in the back in between two students named Lexi and Roger. The tardy bell rang, and I assumed that the students assigned to be seated next to me were going to be absent. I would understand if they were new and did not know how to find their class, but who would be tardy on the first day of school?

Just then, two students walked in and slumped into the chairs next to me. The girl, who I assumed was named Lexi, was wearing a black shirt depicting a band I did not recognize. She had a square face with intimidating eyes and long brown hair that was stick-straight. Her expression was incredibly unenthusiastic. She had a big frown on her face and tired eyes. *We haven't even done anything yet; why is she so mad?* I wondered. The other student, who I concluded must be Roger, was wearing jeans and a solid color maroon t-shirt. He had curly short black hair and a slim face. He wore a bored expression and had terrible posture. I felt like such a goody-two-shoes next to the two of them.

It was quickly apparent that Lexi and Roger were friends and also apparent that they had no respect for others. Throughout the next few months, I noticed them making what they thought were subtle faces at each other whenever the teacher made a joke. They whispered about students in the class, and constantly stretched behind me to talk to one another. They were not afraid to toss jackets, notes, gum and other items to each other behind the back of my chair, and sometimes even directly in front of me as if I wasn't there. It was clear that they either didn't notice their surroundings, or just didn't care. I tried my best to pretend that I didn't notice them, either.

Lexi and Roger constantly whispered during class and would text on their phones during lessons as well. Their behavior made it hard for me to concentrate on learning science, and my grade began to reflect the distractions I was facing. Nevertheless, after a couple of months, I became very skilled at ignoring their frustrating behavior—mostly because I was afraid to speak up, fearing retaliation. I was so scared that if I said something to the teacher, their behavior would get worse.

Lexi had a mean sense of humor, and Roger usually followed behind her with comments of his own. One of their favorite things to do in class was to shout what they thought were funny jokes and insults at classmates during our open discussion time. I didn't understand many of their jokes, but based on the reactions of their victims, I gathered that what they were saying was inappropriate or even vulgar. I felt uncomfortable for all the people who laughed awkwardly at their jokes, and felt bad for all the people who sat in silence as Lexi and Roger poked at them over and over again. I was becoming really sick of it.

One day, another student two seats down from me decided to try to joke back with Lexi and Roger. I couldn't hear exactly what he said, but after Lexi fired a couple of comments at him, he said something back to her, and it backfired hard. Within seconds, Lexi was tearing into this student, calling him names and making fun of him while Roger laughed. They were able to get the entire row of tables involved: everyone jumped on the bandwagon and was intent on destroying this kid. I was so overwhelmed. Everything within me was telling me to say something, but I was so scared of what might happen to me. If I said something, all of the energy daggers would be redirected toward me and I would become their target.

At first, I made the decision to just try to ignore the situation and bury my face in my homework. As I picked up my pencil, I looked up and saw the student's face. I recognized the unmistakable look of utter defeat and helplessness. He tried to act like he couldn't hear them, but his face was turning a pinkish shade, and his jaw was clenched as if he was going to shrivel up into a tiny ball any minute.

I felt guilty about trying to hide, and the feeling of needing to do something about the situation filled my entire body. I stiffened up, took a deep breath, and angled my eyebrows. In the midst of the chaos and laughter, I shouted at Lexi and Roger, "Can you stop bullying him? Please?" There was a shocked moment of silence throughout the classroom as everyone stared at me. For a moment, I felt so empowered! Unfortunately, that miraculous feeling did not last long at all.

I saw Lexi widen her eyes and puff out her chest, and my body was flooded with fear. "Excuse me?" she scoffed. Lexi took a deep breath, and I prepared myself for the approaching storm. I was saved momentarily when my teacher announced, "Okay, everyone, class discussion is over for now." Lexi looked at me and went silent, eyes still wide, and slowly moved back to her chair. She was quiet for the rest of the seemingly endless class period. I looked over at the student who was recovering from their abuse, and smiled at him. He was fully aware of my sacrifice, but he sat there, eyes shiny with tears, silent.

I walked into class the next day, hopeful that the events of the day before would be water under the bridge, but my heart sank as I saw Lexi's and Roger's belongings spread out across my desk and their feet up on my chair. I took a deep breath and started my walk down the row of desks. I noticed they also had their backpacks open on the floor, which blocked the path. "Could you please move your stuff?" I chirped. They slowly moved their items off my desk, but were silent and hit me with a death stare as soon as I sat down. I could cut the tension with a knife. I wanted to be anywhere else but in that classroom.

That week quickly became torture. Lexi and Roger refused to speak to me during table discussions and avoided looking at me at all costs, but their focus on me never waned. I noticed my pens and pencils were disappearing, and one day, I found my phone, which had been safe in my backpack, sitting in one of the classroom drawers. I tried my best to remain strong and work around them. I kept my backpack in between my feet under the table, I was constantly "distracted" by my homework, and I limited the number of times I spoke or answered questions in class.

As the school year went on, they began intensifying their reaction to my heroic day. They mumbled that I was a "b*tch" under their breath, which sadly was the nicest version of my name I had heard from them. They hid more of my belongings in the classroom drawers whenever I stood up from my seat. They encouraged their recruits to yell at me and call me a "piece of sh*t" in the hallways as I walked to classes throughout the school day. Every day, I noticed more and more people actively trying to avoid me. After each class, I would find gum wrappers lodged in my hair and pieces of tape stuck to my back.

Despite my growing frustration at the ongoing assault, I was surprised to realize that it didn't entirely matter to me on a deeper level. It was stressful, but every time I looked over at the student I had protected on that day, I remembered what his face looked like when he was being bullied and felt relieved that I had stood up for him. Of course, that feeling didn't stop me from walking onto the campus, feeling hopeful that someone would stand up for me as well, as I had done for another student. Unfortunately, I found that no one else was brave enough to stand up to Lexi and Roger and risk enduring the middle school torture I had brought upon myself.

As the bullying continued, I began to feel defeated. My grades reflected my mounting stress, and the only tardy I ever received in middle school was when I decided to walk around the entire classroom building to avoid passing by Lexi on the way to my class. My intention had been to make some peace in the classroom to protect a bullied student, and it was now a living hell for me to endure. Although I really wanted it to end, I still harbored no regrets about what I did that day.

The school year finally ended, and I had a much-needed break from the constant insults. After summer vacation, eighth grade rolled around, and I wondered whether I would return to the same retaliation I had experienced the prior year. I hoped Lexi and Roger had taken the summer to cool off from our science class and would leave me alone. Miraculously, even though Lexi and Roger were still at the school, I never ran into them, and I never heard another word about my attempt to shut them down. Everyone else seemed to have forgotten about it as well, and the bullying had stopped. It felt like a breath of fresh air!

On a bright spring day near the end of eighth grade, I was finishing my lunch when I was approached by the student that I had stood up for on that day in seventh grade. He was walking with another student from the same class. He told me shyly that he was really grateful for what I did for him and that he felt bad about what happened to me after I stood up for him. The other student told me, "There were a few of us in the class that wanted to say something, but we were too worried." I nodded my head and smiled back at him. I didn't really know what to say. I was just glad that they noticed my efforts!

They began to tell me about a number of things that happened in their classes in the months after the fall semester ended. They told me about how several people who were there on that fateful day in my science class had started helping another student who was being picked on in their math class, standing up for her and telling others to stop bullying her. As they told me the story, I gathered that their situation definitely was not as extreme as what I endured, but that didn't matter. I felt that what I did that day created a wave of strength that was passed on to others. It made me happy to hear that they felt empowered to stand for others as well after watching me do so.

I asked myself later why empaths are willing to stand up for people even when they know they might be torn apart afterward. I came to the conclusion that even when I was at my lowest, I still would not have changed the decision I made that day. I felt that it was my mission to protect others and encourage people to stand up to bullying throughout my education, and my mission was clearly accomplished based on the stories that my classmates told me.

I would certainly rather be someone who stands up to bullying and takes the hit for others than someone who sits back and watches others be annihilated. Empaths are unsung heroes, and although I have sometimes taken quite the emotional beating, I am incredibly proud of the brave person I was and still am today and what I have inspired others to do as well. Being an empathic person may be overwhelming at times, and it may require a thicker skin—but given what we can do to change the world, being an empath is a blessing.

CHAPTER

Seven

Being A Light Hummer:
A Pathway Through Emotions
By Shirley Hilzinger

Shirley is an intuitive energy practitioner currently living in Sedona, Arizona.

She came to this work by a circuitous route. Her formal education led her to become a nurse practitioner. However, she always knew that healing was more than just working on the physical level. Through books, seminars, and help from many people, she began integrating all aspects of herself: body, mind, and soul. The system that has made the most significant and longest-lasting impact is her spiritual and emotional work.

It is Shirley's honor to be able to now assist others in using these methods to access their higher selves and integrate more of their soul presence into their lives. She enjoys sharing these techniques and insights in as many ways as possible, including writing and speaking. She also enjoys spending time in her garden, hiking with her husband, and traveling to visit family and explore new worlds.

Shirley can be reached through her website at www.hilzingerharmonics.com or via email at shilzinger@hilzingerharmonics.com.

Chapter 7

Being A Light Hummer

By Shirley Hilzinger

Y OU AND I ARE light and vibration. Before we took on our denser versions of light and sound, aka our bodies, we were waves of vibration. We were pure potential waiting to coalesce. The cells in our bodies still live by this vibration, communicating within each cell with electrical impulses which correspond to light and sound. *We are Light Hummers!*

Thus, we are in these bodies of various sizes, colors, and shapes with unique personalities and experiences. However, this distinctness of self can make us feel alone and separate. The human experience doesn't often feel like light and sound. To remedy this feeling, we look for validation and belonging in the world around us, first through our families of origin and then through other groups and systems: school, work, and religious organizations. We crave that connection.

But typically, as we look outside ourselves for connection and stability, we lose parts of the self to maintain membership in these groups. As a result, we suppress or hide aspects of our light hummers, disregarding our unique vibration in the hopes that we can align with the group or person. Thankfully, our light hummers never disappear. We've only lost the connection. Such was the case with myself.

As well-meaning as my parents were, they were ill-equipped to deal with emotions, theirs or their children's. My parents expected me to be a good girl and to know and follow the rules. So, I aligned myself with the energy around me, staying under the radar as much as possible. Observe and copy, observe and copy: repeat. *My parents won't like me if I rock the boat.* It was then that the first veil came between me and my light hummer.

And then school started. I loved school, but there were times. In kindergarten, there was a boy that sat next to me. He looked rather like an elf: small, short hair, ears a little pointy. One day he pulled my chair out from under me. I fell hard on the floor. I was more than a little mad. It hurt, and he laughed at me, making me feel vulnerable and embarrassed. Left to my own devices, I would have punched him. After all, I was the middle child between two boys. But knowing that anger, and indeed action from the anger, was not a sanctioned response in school, I could only give him a little 5-year-old girl death glare and suck it up. *Teachers won't like me if I make a scene. Other kids won't like me if I can't take a joke.*

As the institutions in my life, church, school, and family structures, did their work to create a good person, the layers of veils piled on, creating further disruption in accessing and expressing my light hummer. *People won't like you if you say the wrong thing or say too much. It's best to be quiet.*

Fast forward to age 15, when I was a sophomore in high school. I was already a quiet, reserved person. At this point, the system shifted from adult-dominated to peer-run. It was no longer about being good but, in large part, about how you looked. Due to an accident when I was seven, I lost my front tooth. It was all dealt with, with a false tooth which worked well until other dental issues got in the way. For six months, I could not wear my front tooth. I spent those six months with my mouth closed. *People won't like me if I don't have teeth.*

By the time I reached adulthood, it was no longer outside people and places imposing rules on me. Instead, I had become my own oppressor, the disruptor of the signal from my Light Hummer, the master at suppressing all those things that people don't like.

Life went on, and I married and had two children. My kids needed to be perfect because I needed to be perfect. I needed to make the perfect healthy meal. I needed to be creative and productive and contribute to society. *I won't like myself unless I'm perfect.* A constant checking, comparing, and always falling short.

The low point came when I became pregnant for the fourth time. All was going well until it wasn't. This was a molar pregnancy—a rare genetic anomaly where the placenta grows out of control and can invade other organ systems. A molar pregnancy functions like cancer, and the treatment is chemotherapy. It was an intense, though thankfully short, nine months of treatment. After nine months of treatment, the worst was over, and I was cured. However, I had yet to deal with the emotional impact of losing a child and being physically sick. *I won't like myself if I cry too much or if I'm too needy. I won't like myself if I can't continue doing all that I typically do, plus manage this illness.*

It all became too much. There were too many layers over my light hummer. I could no longer access my uniqueness, my glorious light and sound. I had lost my connection to my light hummer. My commitment to these veils, the limiting beliefs, sabotaged my growth and expansion. One step forward, two back. Two steps forward, one back. I felt abandoned by everything in which I had put so much stock. I was depressed.

With prodding from my husband, I began dismantling the veils, removing the layers, and reconnecting to the light and vibration of all that I am. I discovered that my emotions are the key to sifting through the veils—moving some, examining some deeply, and even integrating some. Each cover was an emotion, an event, or a feeling I had yet to address fully. Acknowledging my emotions and bringing awareness, compassion, and forgiveness to my emotions and the situations around them allowed me to see the veils for what they were. At times I didn't even know where the emotion had come from, but yet it was there. Tuning into my emotions showed me all that wasn't truly me and allowed me to remember the light and vibration.

Every time I disengage a veil, a remarkable aspect of my light hummer returns to me. I've welcomed back a fairy with a stubborn streak, a goddess with a rainbow scepter, and a strong leader with a sense of direction, among many other aspects. Yes, surrendering the veils of the known and comfortable allows so much more to shine through. How bold is that?

Realizing those stories, rules, and beliefs were not mine was the door opening to boldness. I no longer needed to listen to and follow along with the program. My original self was not all of those things that I thought they were. I am no longer required to be the perfect human. That was the mental ah-ha moment.

The pathway to rediscovering our light hummers, our bold-ness, is found in and through our emotions. This level of change comes from clearing and integrating the emotional aspects of all the programming and life experiences. The feelings tie us to the programs and leave us stuck with old patterns. For example, we feel joy when we get praised for toeing the line, making the grade, or getting the coveted job. Yet, we keep returning to get more of that emotional hit without really being able to maintain it within ourselves.

I was in middle age when I discovered the power of my emotions. I hardly knew I had feelings or was allowed to

have emotions, much less what to do with t
understood their connection to my health, we'
inner life.

Armed with the information that the human brain registers
the five basic emotions of *anger, fear, love, joy, and sadness,*
I began writing down every day when I had experienced
each of these emotions. Perhaps it was a burst of anger at
being cut off in traffic, sadness that I missed a phone call
from a friend, or the tender feeling of love when putting the
kids to bed. I began to notice *when* I felt these and *where*
these emotions landed in my body. Of course, these five
emotions can combine to create more complex emotions,
such as jealousy. Jealousy is a combination of anger, fear,
love, and sadness. It is easier to identify our emotions when
we break a more complex one down to one of the primary
five emotions.

As I became more comfortable identifying and accepting
my range of emotions during an average day, I started tack-
ling the more significant events in my life. I saw a pattern
emerge in how they flowed through me.

When dealing with bigger, more extreme versions of these
five basic emotions, I developed a method for working with
and through them. It has five simple steps, and when practiced with everyday emotions, we can better prepare for
their weightier versions.

BE BOLD

Step One: Name It

Name the emotion you are experiencing using one of the five categories: anger, fear, love, joy, or sadness. Then, choose the primary feeling that you noticed, even if others were also present.

Step Two: Don't Blame It

Don't blame your feelings on what other people have done or even the circumstances of what happened. For example, the driver that cut in front of me did not make me mad. Instead, I responded to the situation with anger. In other words, take responsibility for your emotional state. Doing this allows us to regulate how we feel and deal with emotions as they present themselves.

This applies to the emotions of love and joy as well. Don't allow your state of feeling love to be dependent on another person or another situation. A person cannot make you feel love. The love you feel is an integral part of being a light hummer. It comes from you, not another person or thing.

Step Three: Don't Claim It

There is a fine line dividing step two and step three; here, we don't want to claim the named emotion as a part of our being. We tend to say, "I am so depressed!" rather than, "I am experiencing sadness." There is a distinction between *being* sad and *experiencing* sadness. Saying it this way allows a bit of distance between ourselves and our emotions. It gives us a chance to examine the situation with clarity. It also keeps the emotional state from lodging in our system and taking up residence.

We should also note where we subscribe a particular emotional state to a person as only who they are. "That Joe is always angry. That's just who he is." There is no room for improvement if we follow this thinking. There is no way for Joe to become anything but angry in our eyes because he *is* anger. If we notice that he is *experiencing* anger, then we can become curious about what's underneath that.

Of course, this applies to our emotions as well. So be curious about the experience of your feelings. Challenge those parts of yourself that you have always accepted as a part of you. Have you always felt melancholy? Perhaps, it is not who you are. Perhaps, it is that you have experienced repeated sadness in your life that still needs to be processed. Not claiming sadness as who you are, opens up a world of possibility. With each veil removed, more of our unique version of the light hummer shows up.

Step Four: Don't Shame It

Do not feel embarrassed or guilty for having a feeling. Emotions are part of the human experience and how we connect our authentic and our human self. Congratulate yourself on feeling an emotion and owning the impact of that emotion, even if it takes time to get the hang of it.

Step Five: Reclaim Your Energy

The physiological experience, the way the chemical and hormones in the body respond to an event with an emotion, lasts 90 seconds. We run through the fight-flight-freeze scenario in 90 seconds unless we continue to replay the situation or create stories around the occurrence. When we spend time reliving the problem, we deplete our energy. Call back your energy from the issue, and you will have more stability and the ability to move forward. You will have the power to be bold!

As I applied these steps to more and more situations in my life, I began to express more clearly my unique version of light and sound. The lost parts of myself returned to the wholeness of my light hummer. Finally, I could connect and fully sense my original self and authentic expression. So, I limit how much I look outside to give me direction. Now, when I tune into my light hummer and wholeness, I see what's happening and what needs expressing.

Next, we are at the point of action. Boldness in all its forms, from stark white leaps of faith to the baby blue of compassion, takes effort. When we take behaviors from a place of stillness, they pack the most power and boldness. It is the action itself that is the reward.

Our culture often associates boldness with going big, being explosive, and making a splash. Going big is a fantastic way of expressing your authentic, uncorrupted original self. Stand on the stage and say all that you need to say. Go for the big promotion. Finish your degree. Change careers mid-life. Cut ties with people who don't support you any longer. All of these actions take a burst of courage and confidence. It takes tremendous strength to end a marriage or stop the wrangling with a sibling. However, if these actions come without a connection to your light hummer, they are not likely to take hold or feel fulfilling.

And for myself, I learned that being bold is being quiet and contemplative. It's a courageous and confident action to embrace the stillness and feel your soul's interior workings. It is the soul that animates your body and life. Shining your light on internal happenings can be just as bold as standing on the stage speaking to a grand audience. We find this amazing self that does not fit anywhere but belongs everywhere in the quiet and solitude.

Being quiet is not the same as being timid. Being timid is keeping quiet from fear of the reaction that your words and deeds might provoke in another. Holding back is based on fear of rejection, being alone, and not fitting in. Timidity is a reflection of all the veils that cover your light hummer. Lacking courage and confidence keep us hidden beneath the veils. At first glance, it may feel like it is you to feel small, but keep looking for more.

Being quiet, on the other hand, is knowing when and where your words and deeds will have the impact that you desire. Knowing that they are in alignment with your authentic self is empowering. By connecting to your light hummer, you will know what needs to be said and done. Then have the confidence and courage to say and do what is in alignment with your interior humming. And there is nothing bolder than taking action from your most authentic self, your perfect compass, the self that is uncorrupted from the original light hummer.

There are an infinite number of ways to reconnect and maintain harmony with your light hummer. Explore any that you seem drawn to investigate. Be bold in pursuing your light hummer. Look inward and feel at home in your body because this is where you belong. Your light hummer is a beautiful, iridescent sparkler. Even the smallest of actions you take are a pebble in the pond that spreads its boldness in tiny ever-widening rings.

You are a glorious light hummer; anything that tells you otherwise is not the truth. Whether you shine big or small, it's all an inside job. May you know *your* light hummer and create *your* boldness.

CHAPTER

Eight

Be Bold. Be Authentic.
Take a Chance.
By Patricia Holgate Haney

Inspired by a love of books passed down by her father, she immersed herself in the written word and dreamed of exploring the world.

With her husband Gary, she continues to explore the world with insatiable curiosity and enthusiasm, reveling in the opportunities to meet new people and share experiences where places from pages come alive.

At home, she enjoys time with her husband and family, which includes two sons, three grandchildren and three great-grandchildren.

After careers in both non-profit and for-profit corporations, she focuses on writing and has been published in numerous compilation books and is currently working on a solo book.

She volunteers for organizations that are dedicated to helping the underserved and ensuring equality for all. Profits for the sale of books on her website are used to provide for the unsheltered.

You can reach her by e-mail at seaglass@phtravels.com
Website: phtravels.com
Amazon: amazon.com/author/patriciaholgatehaney

Chapter 8

Be Bold. Be Authentic. Take a Chance.

By Patricia Holgate Haney

H AVE YOU EVER BEEN afraid of stepping out of your comfort zone? I know I have. I have had to push myself many times; I still do it.

We must step out of our comfort zones or our own self-imposed limitations. We need to push ourselves to live authentically.

I have always been afraid to show my vulnerability. I was positive that it made me appear weak or not worthy. I try to reach down deep to find the courage to be my true and authentic self. I am learning to honor and be respectful of my emotions. My boldness may not be the same as yours, but we all have the intellectual well we can reach to find our authentic selves.

I remember going through a relationship transition, a breakup. I was afraid of anyone knowing I had failed again.

Yep, that's the way I looked at it. Not that I had been wrapped up in a narcissistic relationship, but more afraid of what others would think because it failed than what it was doing to me. My ego, heart, and soul were crushed, yet I kept trying to fix the relationship. I was afraid I would be considered a quitter, someone who kicked someone down when they were out. I immersed myself in work and was rewarded with respect and trust to work on projects. I was very successful at work, but my relationship was a mess.

The person was an excellent gaslighter, and it compounded my own insecurities. I was lost at what to do other than work incessantly and avoid home life as much as possible.

I remember when I was put into a last-minute situation at work. I was asked the night before to lead a discussion and presentation on a procedure I had not had much experience in.

The group was about 60 upper management and some team leaders. I stepped up to the front and began presenting the material I had prepared. Last minute power points and handouts I had put together at home and printed in the office. Inside, I was trembling; I was trying to maintain my calm. I dressed to impress in my best suit and felt I was doing an excellent job helping the attendees understand the procedure. I started to breathe and loosen up, and then it happened.

One of my colleagues raised their hand and said, "I have a question." I gulped and prayed that I would not be stumped but was ready to give it my best. Her question, however, was, "Why are you wearing two different shoes?" I was confused. Then I looked down and saw I had put on two different patent leather pumps.

One was dark brown with a square toe and a squarish heel. The other was dark navy blue with a rounded toe and a chunky taller heel. How the heck did that happen?

The following words out of my mouth gave me the confidence to handle embarrassing or difficult situations. I found myself saying, "I am so glad someone finally observed the difference." I continued and stated, "I was afraid I'd done all of this for nothing. When we are working on a project, we need to be observant because the little, seemingly insignificant differences may hold a solution." As I looked at the audience, I found that the person who had questioned it was slightly aghast, and my district manager was beaming.

He came up to me later and said he was impressed with my ability to handle a problematic situation and told me to hold on. He had some other projects for me.

My confidence was boosted, and I was glad I took the challenge, proud to have stepped out of my comfort zone. The next thing that happened was that I was recruited to be part of a national project in Dallas. I took the bold step to go there as a problem solver. I would be living in Dallas during the project. The unknown was frightening, but the step took me to a new level in my career.

I had moved to Phoenix from California a year before to continue my employment since the locations I worked in

California had been closed. Also, my eldest son and his wife and children had moved there.

The project only had some basic parameters; the team, which had been recruited from across the US, to identify the issues and then come up with solutions to solve them.

Distance from the relationship I was in would give me a better perspective. After a year on the project, I returned to Arizona and went into counseling instead of letting someone else dictate how I felt. It was scary to admit I needed help. My counseling showed me that I had all the right instincts deep within the relationship, but I didn't have the confidence to believe in myself.

I had found passion in my work, and by eliminating the destructive relationship, I was able to open myself to other new opportunities. Was it scary? Yes, but it was cathartic.

I found that it was okay to ask for help. I surrounded myself with a supportive team of friends; it took time, but the wait was well worth it. Having a group of friends and mentors with whom I could share my doubts and dreams out loud was a fantastic experience. No more hiding behind my self-limiting insecurities.

Others don't always see us as we do ourselves when we look in the mirror. I still have days where I am overly critical of myself. Sometimes those deep-rooted insecurities show up when I am going to be in the presence of people I respect. I must stop and do a little self-talk and get myself out of that negative way of thinking. If I appreciate those individuals, why do I question if I belong in the group? Old self-talk and habits creep in. I've learned to put my shoulders back and go to the events with those I respect and not place my insecurities in the way. I have had many unique experiences in doing so.

I began to realize I didn't need to check all the boxes. I am embracing myself. Authentic and following my dreams.

Also, I've learned that the failures that haunted me, marriages, job losses, and relationships are those things that have made it possible for me to stop saying "what if" and instead say "let's do this."

I am okay with less than 100 percent success.

I try not to set a goal. My goal is to just do it. If it results in 90 percent, that's great.

Put me out there. Sometimes it works better than others, but I am satisfied with the fact I tried. If I hadn't at least tried, I would always be wondering what if.

I work on eliminating all negative self-talk. When negativity creeps into my thoughts, I pull out my gratitude journal. I also love to look through notes and cards I've been sent where someone took the time to tell me kind things.

I never really thought of myself as bold. It sounds like such a scary word. The moments of boldness may be few and far between, but I relish them. Those moments would bring joy and a sense of accomplishment, even if they didn't turn out as I wanted or expected. I tried.

I am a work in progress. I try to step up and go out on edge in life. I want to push the limits of what may be possible. I want to at least go out and try to make my dreams come true.

I want to live my life by speaking and acting in ways that are true to me. I want to be courageous.

I'll get back up when I fall, though sometimes that is difficult. I try and surround myself with people who believe in me. Getting back up and even asking for help are signs of being bold.

We must remind ourselves of our capabilities. Learn from our mistakes. Make entries in your journal as reminders of what you have accomplished. Those kudos will give you encouragement if you need it.

Priorities can change, and that's okay too. Stay true to yourself and show how you want to present yourself. You don't want to be the person who says, "I wish I had." Be the person who says, "I gave it my best shot, I learned from it, and I'm going to keep trying because I know I can."

Write down four things you want to try to boost your confidence.

I keep these quotes in my journal as well as others.

"Remember that everyone you meet is afraid of something, loves something, and has lost something." —H. Jackson Brown, Jr.

"Twenty years from now, you will be more disappointed by the things that you didn't do than by the ones you did do. So, throw off the bowlines. Sail away from the safe harbor. Catch the trade winds in your sails. Explore, Dream, Discover." —H. Jackson Brown Jr.

And finally,

"Instruction for life. Consider that great love and great achievements involve great risk. When you lose, don't lose the lesson. Follow the three R's: Respect for self, Respect for others, and Responsibility for all your actions. Remember that not getting what you want is sometimes a wonderful stroke of luck. Learn the rules so you know how to break them properly." —H. Jackson Brown Jr.

Be bold. Laugh in the face of fear. Hold your head high and walk toward your goal with a purpose. It's not just a hobby. It should become a way of life, a lifestyle, and ingrained within you so you can just do it and be bold.

Boldly go where you have never gone before! This variation of a famous *Star Trek* quote says it all. Let's discover our own new and uncharted territory. Step outside of your comfort zone. Don't let your self-doubt and negative talk prevent you from trying. It may not work out, but you can take a lesson to the heart of how to approach it the next time.

Be bold. Be authentically you.

CHAPTER

Morning Routines
By Lib Keeter

I am a perpetual student and a teacher. I developed my own curriculum directed towards our children remembering the lessons of our planet based on my adventures as a volunteer health care worker in South Africa and Swaziland. I am a certified Results System practitioner and Instructor with the former Institute of Higher Healer developed by our beloved deceased Margaret Fields Kean, Body Awake

Yoga Instructor and Remote Healer with Dr. Sue Morter's Institute. I have worked on boats in the Dominican Republic and the Bahamas taking people swimming with Humpback Whales and Dolphins in the wild.

Reach Lib Keeter here, nomcebowhale@yahoo.com or at 336-964-5790

Chapter 9

Morning Routines

By Lib Keeter

"RATHER THAN INSIST ON being the sole author of my life, I invite the collaborative forces of the universe. Synchronicity, coincidence, reinforcement, and serendipity—these are friendly companions which speak to me clearly of higher realms." —Julia Cameron

There is one for every stage of life. Every purpose is to be lived out. This has been my experience throughout my life as far back as I can recall. It sets the tone for my day in the unfolding of each adventure that comes my way.

Virginia Beach, VA. 1990. I wake up each morning in Moonshadow, my grey 1985 Camaro. I take the towels off the windshield, carefully unwrapping the edges from around the sun visors, and unstuffing them from the corners of the dashboard. Then I roll down the windows, removing the towels draped over them to shade myself in my dream chamber. Last, I remove the back hatch cover and step out into the ocean breeze in my ocean swimming attire. I walk down the beach to meet the local pod of dolphins. I walk ahead of them and swim out to greet them. I can hear them underwater before I can see them.

This is what led me to meet a woman on the beach who needed a ride to Smith Mountain Lake, VA, to take a 14-day course on healing called the Results System. It was being given by Margaret Kean, who brought it back from a near-death experience. We climbed aboard Moonshadow and journeyed from the flatlands to the hills. Upon arriving at the Institute for Higher Healing, we were greeted by a smiling, shiny Margaret. My plans were to drop my new friend off and head back to Virginia Beach to decipher my next steps. For I had recently come out of an 11-year relationship/marriage. I created and dismantled a home-school, which I named Kaleidoscope School Without Walls, where most of the studies took place at the Association for Research and Enlightenment, the Edgar Cayce Foundation. This all happened around having to resign from teaching in the public school system as a physical education teacher because I missed passing the National Teacher Exam by a few points, seven times.

When Margaret laid eyes on me, she said, "What took you so long to get here?" I would later discover at a gathering of the priesthood of Melchizedek in front of hundreds of people that she had seen me in one of her near-death experiences. She invited me to join the class. Having not a dime to my name at the time, I explained that I could not, to which she replied, "Your class has already been paid for by the previous class. That is how I work. I do not offer a class until it has been paid for. We work on a donation basis." Long story short, I stayed for the next decade.

Morning Routine

Swaziland, Africa. 1996. Every morning. I go for a trot on the same route, by the cornfields, around the sugar cane fields, the banana plantation, and back around the pineapple fields. It is a time of peace and adventure for me. I talk out loud to God and my ancestors, as well as friends and family who are sleeping back in the States and Canada. All this lifts me, allowing me to be in the heavenly instant. Many birds fly around me. The sound of the flapping of their wings reminds me of my angel self. My favorite part is greeting the women in the fields, hoeing the weeds out of the corn and dropping the banana trees that have filled their bunches. I speak in Siswati, "Sanibonani," which means I see you all. Bowing slightly in the herald, the day position, hands a little above the head. They smile big and, in unison, sounding like a song, respond with, "Yebo, sissy." Yesterday I was making my way up the red dirt road when I heard an extra word spoken, "Ngiyakutsandza." I turned around and walked to them and said, "Sorry, mama, I speak little SiSwati" a big smile came over all the women, and the words, I love you, were spoken to me, making my whole body smile. I bowed and said, "Ngiyabonga kakhulu," thank you much, and I love you too, "Ngiyakutsandza."

We work mostly out of the boot of our white Toyota Cressida. It would be nice to have a 4-wheel drive to make getting around the mountainous areas where the woman we treat for leprosy lives. The first time we went to meet her, the family had to set some old tires on fire to crack open and move the rock in our path. There is always someone who speaks English for us to treat the large groups of people; women, children, babies and the partners of the women needing to also be treated for an STD or go get tested for HIV/AIDS. Many times, the men would come with sores on their penis, wanting to know how they can get their penis hard more times. Margaret uses the Results System, checking the physical, nutritional, emotional, electrical and spiritual areas of the person's life. She would use me as a surrogate to see where they were weak and strong using the kinesiology of my thumb and finger.

Jenny, the owner and founder of Gone Rural, meets with groups of women in rural areas to give and receive love really. This is in the form of collecting grass (a task done by another group of women at her shop) give the grass back to the women to weave into baskets, mats and rugs she then sells in various shops around Swaziland and South Africa. Today we joined her in the gathering of the baskets and Christmas party for the women. We drove to one of the most beautiful rural areas of Swaziland, way in the mountains. We sat in our car, Yota, filled with various supplements, worm medicine and STD concoction of antibiotics. And observed as the women gathered themselves in a circle. The energy of strength of these women in a circle is palpable. They sing praises after the business at hand is discussed. Next, we are called over and introduced as healers who have come to give another sort of Christmas gift. Jenny began to give out sticky buns and fills their cups; they were told to bring with them juice and given little bags of candy. First, the leader of the women came with a big smile on her face. She lifted her skirt to reveal red bumps all over her upper thighs. We gave her love in the form of a salve. She danced around before the other women holding her skirt up to show what she had been given Muthi for. That is when the other women formed themselves in a line to be treated. The clouds began to well up, umbrellas popped up, and the rains came. The women stayed, and so did we. Several women appeared like guardian angels opening their umbrellas and angling them so that the rain did not hit us or the medicines. We treated them one by one, giving them love in the forms of worm medicine, vitamins, salve, and STD antibiotics, along with some straight talk about the sacredness of sex and Swazi men. As we tested for weaknesses in the body, we recorded their name and what was given and packaged their Muthi. Amazing Grace was shared by all. Trembling from the cold winds and rain, fingers and toes numb, the last woman was treated, and we departed, floating down the mountain singing praises in joyful bliss that made the green of the foliage seem greener, the life in the huge rocks come alive, and we each pondered the smiles given and received. The question Margaret and I woke with the following morning was what to do to empower the women to stand strong in the face of the men. To have the courage to look at their penis before it enters their sacred chamber. To insist on them wearing a condom to protect themselves from the disease despite their clever tongue that declares they have been loyal when their penis (which they perceive as another life besides their own) is dripping with sores from entering time and again woman after woman in a disrespectful manner. What to do? What to do? What to do?

Knysna, South Africa; Election of Mandela Day 1994

Down in the streets, there are lines of mostly women and children camped out with their mealy meal, mangos and roasted corn. The smell is grounding and wholesome, the way you feel when something great is about to happen, and you feel safe and at home. They have traveled for miles to get to the nearest voting station. The ballets have been delayed for a few days. I ask one mama how she feels about the delay. Her response was, "I have waited all my life for the opportunity to vote. What is a few more days?" Nelson Mandela, what an example of forgiveness. Once elected, he and Desmond Tutu arranged the truth and reconciliation trials for the white South African police and military, which went into townships and shot dead numerous black South African women, children and men for power and the color of their skin. The response once leadership shifted, the whites responsible for the killing had to confess before the families of those they had taken, look them in the eye and say they were sorry. Once done, they were given redemption.

Morning Routine

I wake, and before I open my eyes, I recall dreams and scan my body for any feelings the night's adventures conjured. I breathe them up and down. I call on the higher realms for support in the day. I then roll over and turn on the amber-beaded lamp and the Sacred World CD. Next, I step onto the yoga mat beside my bed, lighting a candle and Nag Champa incense. I offer the Native American prayer of the 7 directions. I put the top of my head on the mat, emptying any debris. I proceed to a headstand, resting like a bat, relieved by my being upside down.

North Carolina, USA Public Middle School

"We are looking for a new Physical Education Elective. We surveyed the students, and that is what they want, something besides being in the gym," said the principal interviewing me for the job. This is the synchronicity that gave me the opportunity to create a curriculum from all the auspicious experiences in South Africa and Swaziland. All the muthi I had gathered in my bones from a decade with the Sangomas (traditional healers, what Americans would call Shamans) and Margaret's applications of her brushes with death for the good of the whole. Now would be my turn to step up to the plate and serve up the creations that flow through. It started out as Survival Fitness and evolved into Nurture Fitness. Each class became a tribe. Each tribe would have teamworking groups. We dug out tribal gardens and grew foods for the organs, glands and systems of the body. We blazed nature trails through the woods in the back of the school. This would be the magic I shared for 20 years. Each tribe has a territory, and each group of 4-5 builds a debris hut. Vines, sticks, leaves, moss, and pinecones are their materials. Nature is the teacher and the classroom. Questions come from curiosities, and so true learning takes place. The heart-shaped ginger catches their keen eye, and wonder turns into touching the leaf, releasing the smell of ginger and all its healing properties that have been taught throughout the ages. We practice yoga and other stress management tools I have gathered in my tool belt. Students now are the children of former students.

Letters left on my desk:

"Dear Ms. Keeter,

You teach us how to deal with stress, and because of it, you help me with stress. You also teach us how to deal with bullying. A friend who was cyberbullied was helped because of what you taught us. I had saved my friend from being bullied. Thank you."

"Dear Ms. Keeter,

I really love your class. You really have helped me have motivation every morning. I think meditation really does help me relax. Thank you so much for your class. I really do love it."

Quotes from the students: "I like the escape of indoors, and fresh air and vitamin D, the insects, spiders, the leaves, and I like fall. I like the fact that we just get to go out, period. It's just a nice change of pace. Nature is nice because it helps you with your mood, makes you feel good, and it makes you not be mad at other people. It feels like a little bit of freedom because you are locked inside all day."

Morning routines are my guides and the guides of our future.

CHAPTER

Ten

From Shame To Sparkle:
Thriving With Mental Illness
By Susan Rae

For over ten years, Susan Rae has been a Life Coach, Healer, and Spiritual Leader of an International Community. Using her original 3Rs System for Manifesting, she helps her clients get unstuck and create the badass, spiritually aligned lives they have been craving. She facilitates her clients individually, in groups, in workshops, and in retreats. Susan is renowned for being generous with her time, wisdom, and talents in supporting others' transformation. She is the creator of the Manifestation Accelerator Program: the MAP to your happiest life. She is widely known for her larger-than-life, positive energy and ability to convey profound love to everyone she serves.

She is an International Best-Selling Author, a Sacred Depths Practitioner, and a proponent of Dialectical Behavior Therapy, with a university education in Organizational Development and Psychology. Following a thirty-year corporate career, earning the title of Vice President of Human Resources at one of the largest hospices in the United States, Susan left the corporate world to pursue her calling to help others on a deeper, more personal level.

Contact her directly at susanraelifecoach@gmail.com or join her Facebook Group, The Spiritual Path: From Stuck To Manifesting Your Abundant Life, by visiting https://www.facebook.com/groups/spiritualmanifesting

Chapter 10

From Shame To Sparkle

By Susan Rae

TWENTY YEARS AFTER MY diagnosis, I am living the life of my dreams! I have experienced mind-blowing healing with my incredible daughter; I have the most loving, healthy, and inspiring partner in the world; I have friends who truly accept me exactly as I am, and I am privileged to serve clients whose brilliant souls amaze me daily with their dedication to creating their happiest lives. And everyone should know that a healthy, beautiful, fulfilling life is within reach, even with mental illness! I'm getting ahead of myself, however. That's the sparkle. Let's begin at the beginning, with the shame.

The Diagnosis

Sitting across from the doctor, with whom I'd become comfortable through several days of psychological testing, I suddenly felt uneasy. I scheduled with her because I was longing for a name for the chaos that had always been my life. I wanted to know what was *wrong with me*. Because my daughter had recently been diagnosed with ADHD, and her psychologist told me there could be a genetic component, I wondered if that was my problem. She also suggested that depression (my diagnosis for years) and ADHD sometimes have similar symptoms. Could a misdiagnosis explain why the years of therapy and medication had been ineffective? The doctor's voice pulled me back from the rabbit hole of thoughts I'd fallen into as we began this conversation about the outcome of my diagnostic tests. She said, "You have a very serious mental illness. It's called Borderline Personality Disorder (BPD)." I was instantly flooded with feelings, which won't surprise you if you know anything about BPD. What may surprise you is that I felt relief.

At *last*, I had a name for the collection of symptoms beyond my ability to manage, control, or cure for all these years. Finally, the erratic mood swings, the inability to maintain relationships, that feeling of not knowing who I am from one moment to the next, and the craving for self-harm had a name: BPD. So much quicker to say than to describe the broken, damaged, and beyond-repair person I believed myself to be. I sat there, lost in my thoughts, until I suddenly realized that the doctor had stopped speaking. She watched me with compassion, and when my eyes met hers, she started talking again.

My test results indicated that I was at high risk for suicide. Unless I immediately contacted a psychiatrist about medication, she would petition me to the hospital against my will. The tears of relief, sadness, and fear turned to terror and shame. Petition me to the hospital? Against my will? I have a daughter at home. She's only nine years old. If I'm gone, who will help her father care for her? (This was a question I frequently asked myself to keep from acting on my suicidal ideations, a question that helped me deny my craving to get free of the seemingly endless emotional pain by leaving this world.) Under the doctor's watchful eye, I made the call, explaining to the psychiatrist that I had stopped my medications months earlier as I was attempting to get pregnant again following a miscarriage. We set an appointment, and I was permitted to leave the psychologist's office alone; no psychiatric hospital for me today.

Life felt surreal as I drove home that sunny afternoon. I immediately connected with my fury about the delay in receiving my diagnosis. More than ten years earlier, I had carried a copy of the DSM-IV diagnostic criteria for Borderline Personality Disorder to my psychologist, inquiring about the possibility that I was suffering from this condition. Without any exploratory conversation, she dismissed my inquiry, indicating that it was ridiculous. Reeling from receiving the precise diagnosis I had asked about all those years earlier, my mind was racing about how much time I had lost because that doctor was unwilling to take the time to diagnose me properly.

My heart ached about the probability that my daughter's life would have been infinitely better those first nine years had I been accurately diagnosed and treated earlier. The brain spins continued, accompanied by churning emotions of sadness, despair, and fear. The shame of being labeled seriously mentally ill was profound, and I heard the ego's voice asserting, "See? You *are* damaged beyond repair!" And while I believed that, to the core of my being, I felt a tiny glimmer of hope because I had a name for what I was experiencing.

That hope led me to explore treatment with the psychologist who diagnosed me and the psychiatrist she recommended. I attended weekly therapy sessions and tried medication after medication. We worked together for five years. And during that time, I experienced some relief but nothing I could sustain. *I did the work*! I took my medication, and much like most of my life, I never quite felt like I had my feet solidly beneath me. For as long as I could remember, I felt like a victim of my circumstances, flooded with emotions seemingly dictated by others' words and actions, my critical thoughts, or events in the world.

One moment, I would feel content, or on occasion, even happy, and then a word from a family member, schoolmate, and later in life from a supervisor might strike me as rejection. Suddenly, I was furious or sobbing. My days were roller coasters of emotion, and my months were plagued with conflict in my relationships. When a friend or boyfriend became unavailable or ended things, I frequently spun out of control, engaging in self-harming behaviors like binging and purging or unprotected sex. Hours (often days or weeks) later, I'd be filled with self-recrimination and remorse and try to win back the friend or lover. I almost always experienced the insanity of extreme thinking, "I'm a good person, dammit! I deserve to be treated better, and if they won't, they're dead to me," and then equally as intensely, "What was I thinking? I am the worst person that ever lived, and I'm lucky they even speak to me. I'm better off dead!" Those thoughts were often followed by what felt like endless fantasizing about suicide, focusing on finding a way that created the least mess and caused me minimal physical pain.

I seemed to have more ability to exercise self-control in the workplace than many people with BPD I've met, but at home, my symptoms were quite present. As a teen, I often screamed and wailed, completely inconsolable, telling my mother I wanted to die. She comforted me the best she could, though most times, a shower and bed were the only options as we waited for the emotions to pass. When I was older and in romantic relationships, I would beg my partner not to leave me after an argument, and when he stayed, falling silent (to protect himself), I would shove my face inches from him and yell, "You will talk to me!" He didn't. Yet, I didn't learn to stop this pattern of behavior for many years. In friendships, I obsessed about being the favorite, best friend, and closest to all the action. One particularly horrible experience occurred in my early thirties when I was friends with two women whose husbands were excellent friends with my husband. We spent most weekends together, the six of us, with our children. Because of my intense fear of abandonment and inability to maintain any stability in my identity, I set about trying to divide the other women's connection so they would be closest to me and I would feel safe. To this day, I am not clear if I was aware of the mission I'd begun or if it was genuinely unconscious, but I gossiped about each one with the other trying to create upset and conflict between them, and one day they discussed me when they were alone together. All the manipulating I had been doing came to light. They never trusted me again, and our relationship ended.

Sadly, I wasn't the only one hurt by my BPD-driven behaviors. This incident is only one example of how my illness impacted my daughter's and husband's lives. In this instance, things changed dramatically for them, too, because we were no longer welcome to spend weekends as a family with our closest friends. The pain and self-loathing that would follow these episodes were nearly unbearable. It was one hundredfold when I saw the pain I caused others and the carnage I left in my wake.

When most of these behaviors continued even after dozens of medication trials and five years of therapy, my psychologist and psychiatrist discharged me. I was devastated. Because our mood lability, rage, and impulsivity can make us incredibly challenging patients, it's not uncommon for people with BPD to be discharged from care. Yet, I hadn't been inappropriate; I had always been respectful and polite with both doctors, and I experienced their decision as a colossal betrayal that left me feeling completely abandoned. The psychologist called me and informed me by phone that the psychiatrist believed we couldn't find an effective medication regimen because I wasn't receiving the proper type of therapy. She indicated that she would no longer be treating me and instructed me to pursue Dialectical Behavior Therapy (DBT).

DBT

I followed her recommendation and will never forget my first experience with DBT, the premier therapy to treat Borderline Personality Disorder. I enrolled in a program at a nearby clinic that offered group therapy in conjunction with individual sessions. Because the group was about to begin when I found this provider through my insurance plan, I did not have an individual session before joining the group. The first group session focused on Mindfulness and included an exercise of describing a rose we were to see in our mind's eye. It felt awkward and unsettling to try to provide the level of detail and observation being encouraged by the therapist, but it was *something* to try. It was something to do besides feeling sorry for myself and contemplating suicide. I left the first group feeling equal parts skepticism and hope. Days later, I had my first individual session with the therapist. She asked about my family history. I outlined for her the highlights (or low-lights, as it were) of my childhood, including a mother who was hospitalized for mental illness, tended to rage at us, and was physically violent. I told this new therapist about my father's alcoholism, his violent sexual assault on me for years, and my desperation to find a way to appease and soothe my parents to stay safe. I looked at her after pouring my heart out, eager for her reassurance that DBT would allow me to overcome my past and find my way to a happy, healthy life. Instead, she *literally* buried her face in her hands, shaking her head from side-to-side sighing loudly. When she looked up again, she said, "I don't even know where to start." I felt like I had been punched in the stomach, and all the air left the room. I had begun the session with optimism. I believed I had finally found the path to happiness in DBT until she imparted to me, with her reaction, that my case was hopeless, that I genuinely was damaged beyond repair. I didn't continue treatment.

Months later, I finally found another DBT program, and after some convincing, my husband agreed that though it was private pay, it was wise to try a new provider. The phrase night and day can't even begin to cover the difference in my experience with the new provider (a husband-and-wife team of psychologist and licensed professional counselor, respectively). The treatment consisted of one group session with homework and one individual session for processing each week. It was life-changing. The DBT model includes four skills-based modules that allow the client to learn to function in the world in more helpful and socially acceptable ways. The modules include Mindfulness, Emotion Regulation, Distress Tolerance, and Interpersonal Effectiveness. Each module teaches in efficient ways the skills that help people with BPD reduce the symptoms that are making their lives unmanageable.

We practiced the skills taught in every group session and received homework to report on the following week. In the individual sessions, we dug deep into the trauma that contributed to the development of the disorder and used powerful treatment modalities such as Eye Movement Desensitization and Reprocessing (EMDR) to promote healing. This program addressed the original trauma, and the habits developed to cope with the pain over a lifetime. I began to experience a shift. For the first time in over twenty years, I was not taking medicine to treat my mental health issues, *and* I was making progress. I became proficient at observing my thoughts.

I learned that if I could manage my thinking, I could often prevent the emotional upheaval that had been a daily part of my life for more than forty years. I had hope! Seizing the opportunity, I doubled down on learning the skills; I became one hundred percent committed to applying what I was learning to create a more stable, happier life. And I did! One year after entering DBT, I felt better than ever. I sailed through significant life changes in the subsequent years because I was more prepared and confident about myself and my future than I had ever imagined. I supported my daughter through her mental health challenges, lovingly ended a 25-year relationship with my husband, and took responsibility for caring for my aging mother, who had developed Alzheimer's. I even became the Vice President of Human Resources for one of the largest hospices in the country!

Life Coaching And My Holy Trinity

I still needed to learn a few more things that DBT didn't teach me before I could live a happy, whole, fully functioning life. While I didn't realize it immediately, first and foremost, I needed to learn of my lovability, innocence, and worth. I'm talking about that relationship with myself that many call self-love. Though I found that statement so often conveyed to people of my generation, "You can't love anyone until you love yourself," nearly unbearable. I became full of rage at that idea because I *wanted* to love others. And loving *myself* seemed like an impossibility. If you have BPD or other mental health challenges or find it hard some days to be clear about your life in general, you have likely had some challenges loving yourself from time to time. I looked for ways to connect with others, practice the skills DBT had delivered, and learn to love. My DBT counselor recommended a book by Dr. Greg Baer, *Real Love, The Truth About Finding Unconditional Love & Fulfilling Relationships*. I discovered a community of people who met regularly to study the book and practice his methods of developing unconditionally loving relationships.

I didn't focus on *loving* myself. I focused on *learning* about myself. Like many of the clients I see today, I had spent so many years living for others in unhealthy and codependent ways that I was no longer aware of my preferences, even in the most fundamental areas. I took time to notice what I liked and didn't like and then learned to make requests about that in a loving, healthy way.

I met a Life Coach who specialized in the practices Dr. Baer recommended. I will never forget our initial meeting; she asked me if I had ever felt loved by someone who didn't want anything from me. I racked my brain, allowing my thoughts to flow to my parents, siblings, friends, and partners. In each instance, I excluded the individual who came to mind. That is until I considered my mother's sister my favorite Aunt. I instantly connected to the love I felt from her and for her, and I remembered the joy and safety I felt in her presence. Tears streamed down my face as I finally responded to the question, "One person. My Aunt Clo. She died when I was six years old. I'm 42 now."

My words seemed to hang in the air as the magnitude of the deficit of loving relationships in my life became crystal clear, which was profound for me. I became even more resolute in pursuing a new pattern in relationships. I spent most nights in those following months connecting with other women with the same focus on learning about ourselves and love. One evening, after a group with like-minded women hosted by this Life Coach, I experienced an epiphany. In an instant, I *knew* that I was lovable. I knew I was lovable intellectually but also in heart, mind, and soul. *Every fiber of my being* seemed to have integrated the Truth of my lovability. The transformation from believing I was damaged beyond repair to truly integrating the absolute Truth that I am lovable changed everything! That isn't to say that I was filled with self-love, and everything fell into place immediately; rather, I knew I was genuinely lovable. Lovability became the first of three foundational concepts upon which I built everything else I needed to create my happiest ever life: my Holy Trinity of lovability, innocence, and worth.

The second foundational concept came to me with the help of a powerful, brilliant Life Coach whom I met shortly after DBT and who's still in my life today. I learned to *experience* my innocence. At that time, seeing myself as innocent didn't come naturally, and it felt blasphemous. Being raised by parents who identified as Christian and hurt me in horrific ways created incredible confusion. The fact that they taught me that I was born into original sin and that I needed to be obedient to *earn* God's love made experiencing my innocence seem unattainable. But I was willing. Somedays, I had to start with being willing to be willing. I implemented tools from DBT like Fact-Checking to use logic to wedge myself into the feeling. I stood or sat on the ground, palms up, repeating, "I am willing to experience my innocence." And I think what finally allowed me to embrace my innocence was the realization that I could *embrace* my serious mental illness through it! In innocence, I could finally release the shame I'd been carrying for years and step into the fantastic gifts in this experience, the incredible treasure that I *am*, BPD and all. I've come to realize that, often, owning something about ourselves that we have a judgment about *without* experiencing our innocence is like having surgery without anesthesia. Like surgery, owning our *perceived* shortcomings or defects is often essential for our health and happiness. Innocence provides the comfort and pain relief needed for a successful, bearable experience, as anesthesia supports surgery.

The third foundational concept upon which I created my life of happiness, joy, and freedom was owning my worth. I learned that The Divine determines my worth. It is intrinsic, and I do nothing to add to or take away from my worth. Further, nothing that is done to me or not done for me can change my worth. You may have heard about or seen object lessons about worthiness. Often a speaker will show a clean, new one-hundred-dollar bill and ask the audience its value. Next, the speaker alters the bill in some way, like crumpling it, stepping on it, or smearing it with mud or some other substance. Listeners are asked again the value of the one-hundred-dollar bill to prove that the worth remains the same. I've always loved those, yet the application and integration felt out of reach until my coach told me her version. She would say that when a cabinet maker builds a cabinet, *he* determines its worth. He knows the cost of the materials and the amount of time in labor spent on his creation. The maker *knows* what the cabinet is worth; regardless of the price other people may *believe* the cabinet is worth. This version of the object lesson has helped me release my need for others to see and validate my worth. I learned that I am worthy of love no matter what and that other people's opinions of my worth are, frankly, none of my business. Knowing I am lovable and innocent has eliminated the need to rely on others to tell me or show me I'm worthy.

An Invitation

Let my story allow you to embrace the magic available in a life with mental illness. As you finish reading this, I invite you to *decide* that you deserve to live the life you're craving; step into the Truth of who you are (even with, maybe especially with, a mental illness). There are many ways to integrate the Holy Trinity of lovability, innocence, and worth as your foundation upon which to build. Finding people who can love you, believe in you, and hold the Truth about you for you when you cannot, will have a profound impact. Check out places that feel good to you, like churches, twelve-step groups, other support groups, and communities with a mission that aligns with you. Leaning into spiritual principles that resonate and using DBT tools (available through a therapist or online) and manifestation techniques can provide another level of healing. You can come *home* to your happiest ever life using a method or system like my 3Rs System for Manifesting that allows you to Reveal past imprinting and programming, Reinvent the way you see yourself and the world, and Receive all the abundance meant for you!

Whatever path you take to get there, join me in allowing *all of you* to be lovable, innocent, and worthy. There is something quite magical about individuals with Borderline Personality Disorder and other mental illnesses. What would be possible if you stood tall in that, sharing your *sparkle* with all the world?

Footnote: For more information on Borderline Personality Disorder or other mental illnesses, visit https://nami.org/About-Mental-Illness/Mental-Health-Conditions/Borderline-Personality-Disorder

CHAPTER

Eleven

Be Bold: Healing
By Desiree Richards

Desiree Richards is a Licensed Clinical Social Worker in Texas who is trained in Eye Movement Desensitization Reprocessing therapy and a form of cognitive behavioral therapy for weight management. She received a Bachelor's in Counseling from Southwestern Assembly of God University. Her Master's degree was completed at the University of Texas at Arlington. Areas of specialty include depression, weight management, and trauma. She personally and professionally understands the importance of health in body, soul, and spirit. Desiree has experience with being a personal trainer and therapist, and grew up going to church regularly. Desiree has dealt with weight management difficulties, including a two-hundred and fifty-pound weight loss, has done a tremendous amount of work on her personal development, and is realizing what it looks like to transform her faith into something more spiritual. Desiree grew up in a Christian environment in a small town in Iowa and came out as a lesbian in 2019. She has concluded that struggles with weight can be closely linked to depression, trauma, and a struggle to embrace our authentic selves. She desires to inspire readers to be *bold* and find healing in body, soul, and spirit. She has worked to establish her own company, Sozo Counseling, which includes clients she sees and a presence on social media. She hopes this chapter is the beginning of sharing her story with the world and helping others find hope and healing in the process. Personal interests include quality time with her girlfriend and friends, adventure, traveling, exercise, personal development, and her two cats.

Email: desiree.richards7@sozocounseling.net
Website: www.sozocounseling.net
Facebook: www.facebook.com/sozocounseling.tx
TikTok: www.tiktok.com/@sozocounseling.tx
Instagram: www.instagram.com/sozocounseling.tx

Chapter 11

Be Bold: Healing

Desiree Richards

"**D**ON'T ASK WHAT THE world needs. Ask what makes you come alive and go out and do it. Because what the world needs is people who have come alive." —Howard Thurman

To be bold. Everyone has their idea of how being *bold* may be defined. I believe being *bold* is to be alive and in the arena of our own lives. It's the client in my office who is struggling to brush their teeth in the morning because the sadness they feel is like a weight of bricks on their body that will not lift. It's the people who try and try again to manage their weight and eat healthy even when it seems like the hope of being healthy is as tiny as a pebble. It's individuals who may have grown up in a home where they were almost forced to believe in a religion that has transformed into finding their spirituality.

Being *bold* has been an adventure of becoming healed in my body, soul and spirit. My physical journey has been about as up and down as the line of a heartbeat on a machine at the doctor's office. My pursuit of wellness in my soul has come with tears, heartache, loneliness and trauma before it became one of triumph and wholeness. My quest for spiritual growth took a one-hundred-and-eighty-degree turn in December 2019 when I came out as a lesbian after growing up in an extremely conservative environment. This is my story of being *bold*.

Healing: Body

Weight management is a topic that some avoid like the plague. This topic has been about as constant in my life as the ticking of the second hand on a clock. I have gained and lost weight multiple times, been on countless diets and exercise plans, struggled with an eating disorder and eventually found a love for boxing. Being *bold* doesn't mean we never take a step backward; it means we never stop inching our way toward becoming the best version of ourselves, the version that has always been there underneath the trials and trauma.

I was about four hundred pounds when I graduated from high school. On the outside, my car and room were covered in smiley faces as bright as the sun in the sky. On the inside, my heart was wounded. Food was my comfort and friend. It had always seemed to be there when people were not. When I felt lonely, I ate. When I felt sad, I ate. Though I have come a long way, I understand that food will most likely be a battle for the rest of my life. To make myself stop eating a delicious chocolate warm gooey brownie is like trying to turn the Titanic around.

I have been *bold* and tried numerous diets. I lost eighty pounds on Medifast, one hundred pounds being vegan and one hundred pounds with a low-carb and high-protein diet. Never really gave Keto much of a chance. Weight-Watchers was good, but unfortunately, I was not consistent with it at the time. No matter what I tried, I'd crave chocolate and cheese, my two favorite foods. I also tried several different types of exercise. I tried dancing, running, walking and weightlifting. I applied to the show the *Biggest Loser* but did not get picked. One day, I saw a Groupon for boxing. At that point, I was 400 pounds. I worried that I'd walk in and everyone would wonder why I was there, make fun of me, or just not want to talk to the heaviest girl in the boxing class. But what I found was a love for boxing.

Exercising six days a week and eating thirteen hundred calories a day for about a year and a half made me drop weight fast. There were weeks when I did not lose, but I had a trainer who would help me if I got stuck. I lifted weights twice a week and boxed three or four times a week. I lost two hundred pounds in about a year and a half. I was featured in the *Fort Worth Star-Telegram, Women's Health* magazine online (https://www.womenshealthmag.com/weight-loss/a19982625/desiree-richards/) and Popsugar online (https://www.popsugar.com/fitness/210-Pound-Weight-Loss-Story-37548825). I applied to be on *Dr. Oz*, but never got chosen. I even became a personal trainer and taught at the boxing gym for a few months, where I lost weight. I felt incredibly good. When you are overweight most of your life, it is such an astounding feeling when you get to a healthy weight. My confidence increased.

I could ride on an airplane without needing a seat belt extender. Roller coasters were no longer a worry. And I could comfortably use a normal stall in public restrooms. Unfortunately, the weight loss did not last long.

I can remember the day as clearly as a cloudless sky. A friend was over at my apartment, a little one-bedroom in Arlington, Texas, home of the Dallas Cowboys. She had a boyfriend and what seemed to be a good, healthy relationship at the time. After she left, I remember cutting up my vegetables for the week during my meal prep. Knife in hand, vegetables on the cutting board and the smell of cabbage in the air. I got mad. I was worn out from doing everything perfectly. Weary of going to church like a "good girl" is supposed to do and following all the church rules. Exhausted from counting every calorie and watching every piece of food I put in my mouth, down to something as small as one single blueberry. I thought that being a "good girl" and losing weight would help God give me what I wanted. Yet I did not have what I had desired my entire existence, a significant other. I broke. I gave up caring about my food and exercise, ate whatever I wanted and gained most of the weight back.

One aspect of weight management that is often misunderstood is food addiction. I had Binge Eating Disorder before it came out in the mental health bible, the Diagnostic Statistical Manual Fifth Edition. Symptoms of Binge Eating Disorder (BED) are eating excessively in a short amount of time, a sense of lack of control, eating more rapidly than normal, eating until feeling uncomfortable, eating large amounts of food when not physically hungry, eating alone because of feeling embarrassed and feeling disgusted with oneself. I have come to realize that BED also meant I was addicted to food. The worst part about food addiction for me is that you cannot go without food. If you have an alcohol addiction, you can stop cold turkey because you do not need alcohol to survive. Food addiction is the weed above ground that can be seen, yet the root for me has always been a hurting soul.

Healing: Soul

I am a Licensed Clinical Social Worker. I work at a counseling center and am starting to see clients through my business, Sozo Counseling (www.sozocounseling.net). I am EMDR certified, which stands for eye movement desensitization reprocessing. I am soon to be a supervisor and have the certification to help other social workers do what I do. While working on my bachelor's degree in counseling, professors mentioned how social work would give me more options in the profession. At the time, being a social worker was not in the cards for me. I had a stepmom in middle school who made me feel like I was the scum of the earth. She was a social worker. I remember she would tell my brother and me that she knew what abuse was and she was not abusive. Deciding to be a social worker was a *bold* decision that I made. It was a choice to take one of the most difficult times in my life, heal from it and help others do the same.

Unfortunately, that emotional abuse was not the only trauma I endured. I used to think I didn't have any trauma. I have never been sexually abused, nor have I ever been in the military. What I have come to learn with EMDR and other trauma training is that an example of trauma can be a kid who spills milk as a child and the parent yells instead of helping them. That kid may learn from that situation that they cannot make mistakes and they certainly cannot ask for help when they need it. Trauma is now known to be stored in our senses, thoughts, emotions and body. Though talk therapy is beneficial, EMDR therapy helps to process all the junk inside us that got stuck when the trauma happened. Therefore some individuals go to talk therapy for years and still have anxiety, depression, eating disorders, low self-esteem and other struggles. For more information on EMDR, you can visit https://www.emdria.org or reach out to me directly with any of the links listed in my bio.

My parents got divorced when I was five. It was ugly. I have a memory of my mom coming out of my dad's house with bruises. Mom died when I was ten. She was in and out of the hospital with Lupus and other immune diseases. I never remember her not being sick. Dad, stepmom, brother and I moved away from everything and everyone I knew when I was ten. Stepmom was emotionally and somewhat physically abusive from ten to fourteen years old. I remember watching the window above the sink at night because she would come up behind me and yell or hit me if I had done something wrong. I felt like I was never good enough. Running away was a common thought in my head. Dad was never around due to what appears to be a limited ability to connect emotionally. Even as an adult, I have attempted to develop a relationship with him. I have now accepted he is not the father I wanted him to be, though I am open to restoring the relationship if both parties are involved. I grew up in a small town where everyone was Christian and I went to a Christian cult for two years in my early twenties. It was designed to help young adults learn leadership and discipleship within the church. Looking back now, this cult had a part to play in some negative ways of thinking that influenced a mental health diagnosis I still cope with today.

Depression is a mental illness that is now more understood and accepted than it used to be. However, there are still many who believe that those who are depressed should be able to just pick themselves up by their bootstraps and stop being lazy. This could not be further from the truth. Would cancer patients be expected to pull themselves up by their bootstraps? When I have had depressive episodes, it has felt like a ton of bricks are stacked on my chest, wanting to eat any food at home, sleeping as much as I possibly can and having countless negative thoughts about myself and loneliness. I am grateful that I have not had a depressive episode in a while, greatly attributed to an anti-depressant that I take and the work I have done in EMDR sessions with my therapist. Many do not blink an eye when taking medication for a medical diagnosis. Mental health medication is the same. Chemicals in our brains can be affected when we have a mental illness and medication can help. Though the medication currently helps me, all the trauma and depression led me to abuse myself more than anyone else ever did.

I despised myself. I remember a friend in high school saying that I was a great person. Inside, I believed the exact opposite. It was impossible to comprehend there was anything good in me, even though I was a great student and friend. That night, I harmed myself. I felt like nothing I did was good enough. I hated struggling with my weight and I was disappointed in how sad I was all the time. There seemed to be no way out and no light at the end of the tunnel. I felt different than the people in the church pews next to me. It appeared as though they had their lives figured out, but mine seemed to be held together by a thread. All of it was connected to my past by pieces of strings much stronger than a thread.

Socrates was a Greek philosopher who once stated "know thyself." A friend of mine once added to that and it has become one of my favorite quotes: "know thyself, manage thyself." Self-awareness is the awareness of our thoughts, feelings and behaviors. Individuals who have experienced trauma benefit from becoming aware, healing and then managing themselves. I became aware by journaling, reading and seeing a therapist. Healing has come mostly through supportive relationships and EMDR therapy. Managing myself has become more productive when I started showing myself the same compassion I give to my clients. Without addressing the trauma, we often fall back into the patterns we are attempting to change. It took a long time to seek out EMDR therapy after I concluded that I had experienced trauma as a child.

EMDR has changed my life. EMDR helps to connect what we know rationally with what we experience in our gut. I always knew that I was beautiful rationally, yet I did not *feel* it to be true. Countless tears have been shed, but I would not have it any other way. I have gone from looking at myself in the mirror and being disgusted by what I see to truly experiencing love toward myself and my body. I have gone through EMDR personally, but I also use it with clients in my sessions. I have witnessed clients make connections they never knew were there, distress levels decrease drastically in a matter of minutes and negatively held beliefs about oneself and/or the world turn into positives. EMDR cannot erase memory, but it does help us process the experience.

Many other tools and resources have helped me turn some of my own negatively held beliefs and behaviors into something more *bold*, healthy and empowering. Finding out my attachment style and researching how to heal from it has done wonders for my dating life. Knowing my love language has allowed me to be loved when I used to think I wasn't worthy of love. Discussing my personality type with a new-found friend, who quickly became a best friend, connected us in a way that I have rarely experienced. Creating a network of support when needed, such as trainers, nutritionists, doctors and friends who share a similar passion for health and fitness. Opening myself up and being vulnerable with those who earned the right to hear my story (shout out to Brené Brown) has decreased the shame and cleared the path for growth. Seeing my therapist has taught me that it's okay to be me, even if that version of my authentic self is outside the box I grew up in.

Healing: Spirit

I was the bible thumper, good girl and high school youth group leader. My major was youth ministry during my first year of college. I was the kind of Christian that would want to go to church any time the doors were open. I went to a Christian version of alcoholics anonymous called celebrate recovery because I thought I had an addiction that was looked down upon by the church, but now I realize is normal. I wanted to attend all the seminars and learn as much about God as I could. I was in the car with my girlfriend this last week and confessed to her how I used to pray for those *gays* with rainbow stickers on their cars. I participated in a boot camp type of event at that cult mentioned earlier, in which I was challenged to push my body beyond what it was capable of and rely on God. This five-day event was full of marching, rolling around in the mud, log personal training, rolling up and down hills, obstacle courses, sleeping on a football field which included twenty-one minutes of sleep one night and dunking my head in a bucket of ice water if I started to dose off in the middle of the night while watching survivor movies.

As I type this, I am listening to my *coming out* playlist on Spotify. It took me thirty- years to realize that I am gay and love women. I grew up in a town in Iowa with a population of twelve hundred people and at least five churches. Being gay was not on my radar, like the radar in Texas when the weatherman says it's not going to rain and then it ends up pouring and the streets are flooded. Coming out was a *bold* process. It started with some questions and exploring. I got on dating apps and switched to woman-seeking women. Met up with some girls who I would never see again. But I will never forget the first girl who I dated for two months. And to make it even more unbelievable, she was married, we were a throuple and most of my interactions were with her. I remember feeling my body shake as I got out of the car to meet her and when she turned around, I saw her face for the first time. When she touched my hair, electricity seemed to flow through my body. We talked for hours, neither of us paying attention to what time it was. Though it was one of the scariest moments of my life, it was also one of the most transformational decisions I have ever made. I would dare call it, spiritual.

Spirituality is important to me, though it has changed. I no longer attend church multiple times a week. My daily activities do not involve an hour of prayer and devotional time with God. Several of my current practices still feel spiritual. When I sit on my beautiful back patio and sip on my protein-filled and sugar-free white-chocolate flavored coffee while my fluffy orange cat Simba enjoys the outdoors and I read a book about self-compassion. Talking with friends about our past lives as regular church attenders and how we have deconstructed our faith and are now out and proud as lesbians. Sitting in my first home on a comfy couch with a candle from bath and body works called cactus blossom flickering on the end table in front of me as I write this. Traveling to the ocean has become one of my favorites. I enjoy going to Galveston, Texas, as often as possible. Gratitude in the morning and evening for the beautiful soul I get to call my girlfriend. Solo trips I've taken to Cancun, Virginia Beach and Costa Rica. Ultimately, I have found that water is a primary place of spiritual connection for me.

To be bold. My life is not wrapped in a perfect box on Christmas day. There are ups and downs like that of the beautiful Dallas, Texas skyline that I love to see when I venture out there, east of where I currently reside in the Dallas Fort Worth metroplex. I still struggle with food daily. I was just talking to my therapist this morning about how I may do a clean eating cleanse before balancing and eating within *myfitness pal* calorie counting. There are events from my past that I am still working to process with EMDR. But isn't that what it's about? Healing and being *bold* is like an onion, happening one layer at a time. Conservative to proud lesbian. Strict low-calorie counting and excessive exercise to a healthier relationship with food. Depression to stable and thriving. Hating my body to loving the pale-skinned, red-headed, curly-haired, kind, loving woman that I am.

It is my hope, with my story of being *bold* in body, soul and spirit, that you are encouraged to do the same. Jumping on this train ride toward healing has been the best decision of my life. Find a personal trainer or nutritionist if you need one. Search to identify what type of exercise you love. Explore what foods are best for your body. Seek out fifteen-minute free consultations with therapists until you connect with one. Read and educate yourself on what you believe about yourself and the world around you. Be *bold* and take care of that body, soul and spirit of yours. I cannot promise that it will be easy, but I can promise that being alive and in the arena of your own life is as rewarding as a gladiator left standing after the battle.

"It is not the critic who counts: not the man who points out how the strong man stumbles or where the doer of deeds could have done better. The credit belongs to the man who is actually in the arena, whose face is marred by dust and sweat and blood, who strives valiantly, who errs and comes up short again and again, because there is no effort without error or shortcoming, but who knows the great enthusiasms, the great devotions, who spends himself in a worthy cause; who, at the best, knows, in the end, the triumph of high achievement and who, at the worst, if he fails, at least he fails while daring greatly, so that his place shall never be with those cold and timid souls who knew neither victory nor defeat." —Theodore Roosevelt

CHAPTER

Twelve

I'm Bold and I'm Me
By GG Rush

GG Rush is an author, Certified Life Coach, Clinical Hypnotherapist and Clutter Clearing Coach. She is a certified Reiki Master and has studied Aromatherapy, Chakra Balancing, Toxic Emotions and the ancient art of Pulse Reading. She has traveled the world solo and will continue her journey to see the world and find herself. GG, aka Gail Rush Gould, resides in Cary, North Carolina with her cat Bella.

You can reach GG at her author website:
www.Gg-rush.com

Coaching website:
www.SacredSparrowSpiritual.com

Chapter 12

I'm Bold and I'm Me

By GG Rush

WHEN I WAS A child, my older sisters used to make fun of me because I had "imaginary friends." I would talk to people that they couldn't see. Therefore, they didn't exist. But for me, they were very real, and they did exist. My friends and I would act out plays and television shows, and books. Alone in my room, I was a star. I was Mrs. Peel from the British show *The Avengers*. Fighting bad guys in my leather catsuit using my karate moves. I was on Broadway. Singing show tunes that I spun on my record player. I was Cher, witty and outrageous, using my hairbrush as my microphone. I was Nancy Drew, who I read under the covers of my bed long past lights out. I was a famous painter, drawing and painting modern art. I won Academy Awards and Nobel Peace Prizes. I married Davey Jones and Donny Osmond, and later Rick Springfield. My bridal veil was my pillowcase. I led a very rich fantasy life, but it all seemed real to me. I was a very skinny and petite girl with braces on her teeth and thick glasses. My sisters listened at my bedroom door and laughed and called me a weirdo. And maybe I was a weirdo, and maybe I still am.

My dad taught me to read long before I started school. It was one of the many gifts of life he bestowed upon me. We often went to the Smithsonian Museums in Washington DC, where I grew up in the suburbs of Northern Virginia. We visited the National Gallery of Art, where my dad introduced me to the Masters. In the museum, we took in the Hope Diamond and the many exhibits. We went to the movies to see classics and popular pictures. I remember the magnificently opulent RKO Theatre. We listened to vinyl recordings of Broadway musicals by Frank Sinatra and Tony Bennett. I was a kid with the tastes of a middle-aged socialite! And I still am. I still love all those things.

I am a big fan of noir movies and classic horror and black-and-white films. I introduced my own daughters to the same things. We spent hours at the art museum and watching old films. And we still do. As I grew into the middle-aged woman I am today, I cherish the genres and classics my father exposed me to. When he was in the veterans' home with dementia, we still talked about movies and art and music. I took CDs to play for him. He listened to books on tape since he could no longer see well enough to read books anymore. I became a big fan of NPR since he listened to the radio so much. We talked about programs we listened to, like TED talks and BBC news.

My mother was very loving and kind as I was growing up. She nurtured my creativity in me. She praised my art and my poems. She has always written poetry and encouraged me to use my imagination and be who I was. At nearly ninety-five years old, she still encourages me. She shares my books and even helps sell them in her senior living complex.

After my divorce a decade ago, I was scared and stayed in a job for fourteen years that I didn't love because I was financially unsecure and terrified of losing my home and not being able to care for my two daughters. Once I was able to get out of debt and feel secure, I began to take classes and study holistic healing. Eventually, I became a Reiki Master, and I now have my own practice.

And as for those so-called imaginary friends, who is to say that they didn't really exist? In my mind's eye, they were very real. These days it could be viewed as if I was talking to people who had passed, and I was able to hear them and communicate with them. Maybe I was channeling before I even knew what that was. Back when I was a child, I was laughed at by my sisters for my ability to leave the "real world" and connect with beings that they couldn't see or hear. But I could see and hear them. As I grew into a teenager, I stopped listening and seeing, so those spirits or whatever they were began to fade. I never got that ability back. But now I am no longer embarrassed by that gift, so I have started to try again to connect to that realm. I haven't been successful yet.

Recently a mentor and teacher told me she saw a huge change in me. That change was confidence. I exuded confidence, and I held myself differently. I held my head high and walked into the room like I belonged there instead of being a little mouse hiding in a corner. I spoke to everyone and laughed and smiled more. It felt great to hear that from someone I admired so much.

Over the last two years, I had the opportunity to participate in Past Life Regression. I was skeptical at first, but my first experience surprised me and scared me a little to the point I asked to be brought back into my body because I didn't know how to process that experience. The subsequent times I tried it I relaxed more and really let myself experience it. I have twice tried being part of a channeling exercise, and I found that very interesting, but I was also somewhat skeptical and reluctant to let it flow. I will continue to try these methods and modalities and open myself up for results to happen. I continue to try new things: writing, painting, studying, teaching, traveling, cooking, and seeing plays and movies. I started experimenting with new hairstyles and settled on a short pixie cut that suited me. A few years ago, I got cataract surgery and had my lenses adjusted, so I no longer need glasses. I changed my wardrobe and wore bold colors and outfits that helped me to feel that confidence. I became a bold woman!

I am now boldly stepping into my true self and loving every minute of every day! Be bold. Be brave. Be yourself!

CHAPTER

Thirteen

Cultural Appreciation
By Kyra Schaefer

Kyra Schaefer is a Best-Selling Author, Award Winning Publisher, Emotional Changework Therapist, NLP Master Practitioner and Clinical Hypnosis Instructor

For over 20 years, Kyra has been a Master Practioner of Neuro-Linguistic Programming and Emotional Changework therapy, teaching workshops and seminars globally. She is the co-founder and president of the Schaefer Institute for Hypnosis certifying students to become professional practitioners. Kyra is also renowned for her work in the publishing arena and is the founder and director of

As you wish Publishing. She is best known for featuring up-and-coming writers in collaboration book projects winning several Amazon awards for best-selling status. You can find her at www.kyra-schaefer.com

Chapter 13

Cultural Appreciation

By Kyra Schaefer

T HERE ISN'T A MORE prevalent core principle in America than the freedom to explore. Many of us love learning about other cultures. We seek education about other faiths, ancient forms of medicine, and body mechanics through Tai chi, Qi Gong, and Yoga. In food, I love tasting Mediterranean, Middle Eastern, Indian and Asian flavors. The combination of a variety of spices and textures stimulates the senses. Discovery is gaining more and more traction in America as we continue to develop our culture, and technology makes observation more available.

Studying, learning about and putting other cultural wisdom into practice helps keep that knowledge alive. We share our insights and wisdom to survive, and if we all look at what has worked for thousands of years, we will survive and thrive much longer on this planet. Not studying or considering other cultures will be detrimental in the long run. It's important to keep knowledge alive in all forms. I feel a tremendous amount of peace around connecting with other cultures, even in the simplest ways. I am not a professor of different cultures. I don't hold advanced degrees, nor have I studied in-depth what I'm about to share. I have simply observed and made meaning from that observation. I hope my insights will be of service as you discover different cultures.

Chinese Rural Renovation

Every night for about an hour or more, I watched a YouTube Channel called *Leaving City*. These videos show Chinese people renovating old rural properties with limited building resources on high-speed playback. As I watched, I saw how they would connect and harmonize with the property. Here are some things I learned by observing more than 700 hours of renovations.

First, the renovators will search through the rubble to find what they can reuse, then clean out the courtyard. Building or rebuilding an entrance into the courtyard is important because they see it as their sacred space's entrance. They make sure this space is clear and that every corner is accessible. There is often a fountain with Koi fish gulping at the water's surface. The result shows us pathways that curve around stone with different styles of gazebos for resting and relaxing. Sitting areas pop up here and there so that you can enjoy every corner of the space. It feels like an extension of the home or, in some ways, even more important. The value of the courtyard is in its beauty and function. Often they will light firecrackers so God will bless the construction and home. The door is usually painted red to help bring positive energy into the home, even during construction.

While all this is happening, they will ensure a proper sleeping space inside or outside with a covered awning. In addition, they will establish a place where they can cook. They may use an outside wok stove or clean up an interior wood-burning stove. This is when they usually plant a garden. They will look for other edible resources and eat or replant them around the grounds. Water will be the next job to tackle, and they will often clean up and fix an on-property well.

With food, water and shelter taken care of, they will spend the next six months renovating. They will fix or tear down the interior or exterior walls and rebuild those using old and new brick and mason over all the walls with mortar and concrete. They rebuild the buildings to be durable. Meaning they seem to consider the home from the perspective of it lasting hundreds of years, which differs from some other cultures that come from the perspective that things can be renovated or torn down in tens of years. This is because this culture is one of the six main "cradles of civilization" that birthed our world more than four thousand years ago: China, Egypt, Iraq, India, Peru and Mexico. The buildings in these cultures are similar in their lasting ways, whereas, in modern America, we see our homes with more wooden frames with mason façades.

When they need a tool, they make it from the items they find on the property. Using renewable resources like bamboo and bamboo leaves, they have a ton of options. I also discovered how they seal the bamboo to prevent mold and bug issues. By heating the bamboo with a blow torch, it will melt the resin in the plant, causing it to turn from a bright green to variations of shiny dark green and rich dark brown colors. Bamboo is one of the most resilient and inexpensive resources in their building endeavors. Not only that, but bamboo is rarely purchased because it is usually found on the surrounding property.

The renovators are rarely alone. Family members often come to help renovate because they want to pass along their wisdom. The home renovation is usually a home that once belonged to someone else in the family. The renovation using the skill of the elders is a form of inheritance, ensuring the family's legacy will be lengthy and healthy.

The helpers of advanced age are unmatched in their skill. You may notice an elder with a long cigarette hanging from their lips as they build elaborate bamboo walls or smooth concrete over brick like the masters they are. They eat, laugh and take a moment to look around at their progress while observing breathtaking views. It's watching people in perfect harmony with the world around them. It's easy to see that the work is hard but worthwhile, and it shows how everything comes together as they learn and grow as one.

What I learned

As I watched these homes come together, I noticed several insights popping into my mind. I would talk to myself for hours about what I was watching. It may sound strange, but it's how I process information. I take what I see and then make meaning out of it as a personal exploration. I create metaphors and draw lines back to fundamental truths that are helpful. I never know if one day I might be able to call on that wisdom to feel more at ease and balanced.

Construction metaphors are interesting because shelter is fundamental to our survival. Recently, a friend of mine who is a construction foreman and drives earth movers every day said something inspired over some beers and barbeque. He said, "Let's say you are one of three people nailing a nail into wood; you all unintentionally bend the nail every time, and then you are the only one who finally learns the right way to do it. You nail the nail straight every time. You try to teach the other two people how to do it, but they won't listen. Do you keep trying to make them do it correctly, or do you focus on your nails being perfect and teach those interested in learning?" That speaks to me in this way; other people get their choice and to try to get anyone else to change is, in this case, like beating your head against a wall. Let them have their experience; you don't have to manage what others do or don't do. Keep being your perfect and wonderful self; everything else will work out.

I will share a few of the multitude of insights that I gained by watching Chinese men and women renovate old rural homes.

1. Beauty is Important: It is possible to get through this life without beauty, but what would be the point? You can work hard, put your head down and get through a project, but if there is no beauty and no creativity, the task is under-whelming in the end. We can tell ourselves we will make things beautiful later. Our friends above have shown us that

beauty can be incorporated into every stage of the project. Beauty is a lasting and natural part of creation.

2. Sharing is Caring: What we offer the world is not only in what we personally share but in how we relay information to others. What wisdom have you learned from your culture that you can share? What wisdom have you learned from other cultures, which by sharing, will help ensure that cultures continuation?

3. Resources: Use what you have; you are gifted and capable in so many ways you may not have tapped into yet. What you don't know, you can learn, and what you need may already be available to you. Look around with new eyes and see what you've been missing.

4. Keep the Basics, Basic: As my coach once said to me, "You have everything you need already within you. You lack nothing and need nothing outside of yourself for your happiness." To survive in the physical body, yes, we do need food, water and shelter, but we also need to love ourselves and recognize that whatever approval or external validation is simply not necessary for our happiness. In fact, we are happier due to making our choices and loving ourselves in our choices.

5. Learn from the Masters: Throughout history, people have come before you in all cultures. Study all the masters, not only the ones in your culture but in others as well. You will find there are more similarities than you once realized. Jesus, Buddha, Muhammad, Moses and more teachers came before us with valid and applicable wisdom. Modern-day

teachers such as Ram Dass, Wayne Dyer, Alan Watts and others have a wealth of knowledge that can contribute to your well-being. Those mentioned here built our foundations to last. Lean into their wisdom as you continue your journey.

6. Build Things to Last: Your life experiences and wisdom are about your soul's development. Yes, the wisdom you leave behind could be remembered for many years, but it's not only about that. I once asked spirit to tell me why I should write books or create collaborations. What was the answer? "It is for your soul's development. It's not about anyone reading or learning from it. When your time comes to leave this life, you will have pushed yourself out of your comfort zone, trusted and moved the needle toward living and expressing your truest self." This is the type of building that is cultivated and lasts throughout eons, your truest self.

There are so many wonderful things to discover in this world, and it's at our fingertips. I wonder what new culture you will learn about today.

CHAPTER

Fourteen

From Borg to Bold
By YuSon Shin

YuSon Shin is a gifted healer, intuitive, medium, speaker, author, and teacher of the healing and intuitive arts based in Los Angeles. With her trademark joyful and compassionate demeanor, she uses her gifts to help people and pets all over the world heal from a wide array of physical, emotional and spiritual ailments. YuSon loves teaching and holds workshops designed to help students awaken their own spiritual gifts and superpowers. She believes everyone has the power to heal themselves.

YuSon is an expert practitioner in a wide variety of healing techniques because she feels there is no "one size fits all" when working with her clients. She utilizes Akashic records and Chinese energy healing techniques to perform past life, karma and ancestral clearings. She is also a practitioner of the Bengston Energy Healing Method and hosts the Los Angeles Bengston workshops. She is a certified Reiki Master, and also uses Integrated Energy Therapy, 5th Dimensional Quantum Healing, Quantum Touch, DNA Theta, and Access Bars. She is the author of six books: *Holistic, Manifestations, Whispers From The Heart, Soul Warrior, The Empath Effect* and *Be Bold.*

You can reach YuSon at YuSon@ShinHealingArts.com and www.ShinHealingArts.com.

Chapter 14

From Borg to Bold

By YuSon Shin

I IDENTIFY AS A female Korean-Borg-American. She/They. As a *Star Trek: The Next Generation* fan growing up in the U.S., I related to some of the methods of the recurring antagonists, The Borg (short for Cyborg), who existed as a Collective, assimilating in order to "raise the quality of life," while at the same time losing their awareness as separate individuals. Fitting in or assimilating is what the Borgs do best, and every *Star Trek* fan knows, "resistance is futile." I am part of the long history of Korean Borgs who have navigated their way to America for an epic adventure and a better life. By epic adventure, I mean working 60-80 hours a week, losing our individuality, and wrecking our health for the privilege of saying that we "made it" as an American. As part of an immigrant family, my parents insisted that I assimilate into American culture, and as a dutiful daughter, I certainly did my best to fit in, and over time, I found myself using the collective voice rather than my own and allowed my distinctive voice fade into the background. However, over the years, I slowly began to find myself again, run my subversive programming in the background, and slowly but surely, took back my individuality, enabling me to break from the Collective.

My first memory of trying to fit in was as a fresh-faced four-year-old when I arrived in Los Angeles from Seoul with my family, and I forced myself to stop speaking in my native tongue. Shortly after we moved to the States, my dad came to pick me up from kindergarten and saw that the teacher had asked me a question. Since I didn't understand her English, I didn't respond appropriately and she hit me. That was allowed in the 70s, a tragic decade for both corporal punishment and fashion. In un-Borg-like fashion, I cried out loud from the physical abuse, and new house rules were promptly implemented. There would be no crying and no speaking Korean. It would be English only. After many years of speaking only English, I was further dissuaded from speaking my native tongue because when I uttered Korean words, I was quickly met with a lot of finger-pointing and laughing.

The mockery and judgment did not outwardly affect me, though. We Korean Borgs are not only enhanced by me-chanical-looking movements and actions mimicking as-similated Americans, but we are also taught to shut down our feelings and emotions so we can endure all the hard-ships and pain-inducing events in life, without slowing down. So even as life gives us equally abundant joyful mo-ments, we don't even pause to celebrate the assimilation of every new species and their respective technologies. We. Must. Keep. Moving. Towards. Perfection.

On *Star Trek*, the humans and other species on the Star-ship Enterprise, with all their curiosity and emotions, don't absorb civilizations but instead explore new worlds and in-spiringly declare their purpose "to *boldly* go where no man has gone before." This is an altogether foreign concept and *does not compute*. As a Korean Borg, I've been programmed from birth to do the opposite. Rather than be a pioneer, I was programmed to follow any one of the proven (and pre-approved) paths to success and I was told to feel lucky that I had these choices to choose from. The choices were 1) lawyer or 2) doctor. Somehow artist and fireman did not make that list.

My Korean family, much like Borgs (and even our friends, the Vulcans), chose to oppress those pesky feelings and emotions, put our heads down and follow vague blueprints from stories we had heard about the most successful indi-viduals that *other* people knew because that was the best way to "make it." Don't be a hero. Don't be different. Don't reinvent the wheel or buck the system. But be better. Be nice. Be quiet. Don't make waves. Don't draw any unwanted attention. Get straight A's. Give it 110%. This was the blue-print and the recipe for success that was provided to me via the intrusive mind-meld method by the Collective, and it was not exclusive to *Korean* Borgs. I hear most American Borgs have also adopted this hive-mind formula for suc-cess. Study hard so you can go to a good college. Go to a good college so you can get a good job. A job is the only way to get security. Get married because you can't be alone. You must find another member of the hive and make more baby Borgs. If perfection has eluded you, then surely your baby Borg will achieve perfection under the watchful eye of the hive and rigid Borg rules. Work for fifty years until retirement. Then you die. Resistance is futile!

Despite my Borg-like mechanics and upbringing, I have been the outlier in my family, daring to go beyond the Collective's boundaries. At first, it was just testing the limits outside the bounds of the rules of the Collective, much like dipping a toe in the pool to see how the water felt. It's been some time now, and I'm proud to say I've since taken the plunge into an alternate universe. Now I can make my own choices to boldly go where no Korean-Borg-American has gone before. I have created my own unique blueprint for success that looks nothing like the one my family planned out for me. My new path was created by me and tailored for me, and me alone.

I have to admit that sometimes being part of the Collective and having my life planned out for me was comforting, much like the satisfaction you get when you color perfectly within the lines in a color-by-numbers book, or when you watch a little mindless reality television, or eat the same bland microwave dinner every week. Yes, it was boring, but on the plus side, I did *not* have to expend energy to figure out what I liked and what I should do because that was all decided for me. Despite all the obvious benefits, it still didn't feel right even after many decades of assimilation. I didn't quite fit into the Collective. It was like hammering an ugly Borg cube-ship into a round hole. Despite many attempts at assimilation and reprogramming, my distinctiveness still existed. This may have just made me a defective Borg, which goes against the Collective's quest for perfection.

As I look back to the point in my life when I started thinking about other options for myself, I can see that I deviated greatly from the successful path that was laid out in front of me as a baby Borg. The path I ultimately took that led me to where I am now was not like the yellow brick road from the Wizard of Oz. It wasn't magical and it doesn't take you to wondrous places to seek the answers you want and need along the way. It would be great if we all could find our Tin Man, Scarecrow and Lion right at the beginning to help us, but life tends to have you cross paths with people who claim to have all the answers but only add to the confusion as you try to find your way. Unfortunately, sometimes we may be let down by façades made of smoke and mirrors. Like Dorothy ultimately discovered, I found I had the answer within me all along.

At times, I took the path less traveled. Sure, I still studied hard in high school, graduated from UCLA, and got the requisite good jobs. But, glaringly against the fold of the Collective, I did *not* get married and have a baby Borg. Instead, I spent decades developing my spiritual practices by taking classes on many healing modalities, intuition, and mediumship on the side and under the radar of the Collective. I didn't want to assimilate the information, but instead, I wanted to experience it. I love learning and helping people, and, as a result, I chose to be an energy healer, intuitive and medium instead of a traditional doctor. This is unheard of in the Borg community.

To satisfy my Borg requirements, by day, I worked diligently for decades in the corporate world in "safe" and "steady" jobs as a real estate and corporate paralegal, which provided security and allowed me to contribute to my 401(k)/retirement safety net. This is what Korean-Borg-American dreams are made of. I did this all while living a double life as a healer by night. So, over the next 10 years, I worked evenings and weekends as a healer after fulfilling my full-time corporate job requirements during the day. Ironically, I was using my Borg superhuman powers of focus and diligence instilled in me by the Collective, to increase my energy output to be able to work two full-time jobs, which have lasted for about a decade. But there are only so many hours in a day and this Borg, unfortunately, also lost a lot of human friends who didn't understand my lack of available time to play and brunch. Much like the Grinch who stole Christmas, the energy-healing work slowly caused my heart to grow a few sizes, and I shed a few tears over the loss of friendships and a lack of understanding of the Borg condition.

Throughout this period of transition, along this path of living a double life over the past decade, I still feel a great deal of resistance within myself. I still find myself triggered by memories ingrained into me since I was a child by the Collective's programming, which does not mesh well with the emotions that are now switched on in my fully functioning heart. Now, as I write this chapter, I am about to embark on the biggest, scariest journey of my newfound human life. I have just let go of the safety net of my "corporate day job" and am finally striking out as a full-time healer and will no longer be living a double life. While I will finally be stepping fully into the person I want to be, I am also faced with an uncertain and unstable path. The excitement of this next stage of my life is coupled with the knowledge that my new full-time occupation will bring its own unique challenges and uncertainties to contend with as well.

In my own process of becoming an individual, I had to continuously work on actively "overwriting" the Borg programming and experiences, which influenced me in order to become my own person with my own unique programming and not just a product of my Collective making the same decisions over and over again. Similarly, humans are shaped by our experiences, but we are also influenced by events that took place in earlier generations. These past events create ancestral blueprints, which are typically shaped by trauma, grief, shame, guilt, hopelessness, and suffering, which all affect us unconsciously during our lifetime. Transgenerational themes are transferred from one generation to the next. Children of parents who are in a certain economic status tend to stay within the range of their parents or a little better. Most people can't jump to version 10.0 without first going through 2.0-9.0 successively through the generations. On a darker note, if we have any traumas, they tend to keep us from moving forward by keeping us in a programming loop, causing unconscious behavior and leaving genetic imprints that can affect subsequent generations.

It can become very difficult for people to break free from these blocks in order to make decisions and move forward.

As a healer, I've sometimes worked with clients who become too dependent on my intuitive sessions so that they are unable to make decisions on their own. My goal is to guide clients to get clarity on what they want and empower them to trust their own personal programming (intuition). Unfortunately, when they resist my guidance to make their own decisions and become reliant on me to make decisions for them, I have had to learn to put up my own boundaries when necessary. As a healer, you want to help everyone, but healers are not crutches, nor are we miracle workers.

Ironically, another challenge I've endured is people questioning the source of my intuitive and healing abilities. I've been accused of receiving my abilities from the Devil himself. I've never met Señor Diablo, but I've even been questioned by my own Korean-Borg-American mother who came into Borg-hood with heavy Christian pre-programming. No matter how many times I thought that programming was overwritten in my mother over the years, it still pops up like Jesus resurrected.

I've also been told I've received my abilities from programming and information which every human has embedded deep within the DNA of our cells, which has been referred to as the God Code. According to scientist and educator Gregg Braden in his book, *The God Code*, some scientists believe it is possible for humans to one day live in a perfect world once humans come to understand that we are all made by the same higher intelligence. While it may seem that the programming of the two sides of me conflict, the end goal may be the same but through different means.

Perhaps the use of my intuition and healing abilities are just enhanced uses of the programming codes God gave me, and everyone has the Code, but not everyone accesses the information. They leave it dormant in their DNA because no one has taught them how to tap into it, and I've simply learned to tap into it. The ones who metaphorically pick up pitchforks and point accusatory fingers while yelling, "It's the work of the Devil!" also want to tell me how to live my life which is worse than the Collective.

The most uncomfortable challenge I face is when people try to put other people with spiritual abilities on pedestals. They misunderstand that those with heightened intuition and healing abilities are regular human beings just like them. I have fought to remain planted firmly on the ground in my eyes as well as in others. I am not perfect. I curse like a sailor because it lets off steam and therefore saves lives. I don't have a 100% success rate in my intuitive work or healing, and I don't believe anyone does. I am a healer who also has health issues, and I will most certainly die someday. Some healers' egos won't allow themselves to show their vulnerabilities and put up an impossibly perfect image, but I prefer to be real. I try my best to maintain self-awareness of my weaknesses and strengths in my goal towards clarity and self-acceptance. When dealing with healing work, remaining neutral is of the utmost importance. However, it is difficult for all humans to remain in this state because we are all invested in specific outcomes in our lives. Any way you slice it, imperfections are not welcome in either human or Borg communities, and no matter how you identify, it is uncomfortable having your flaws highlighted in public.

Simply being, including being comfortable with my perceived flaws and trusting the process also took, ironically, leaning into what I also believe is the God Code.

The most immediate personal challenge to me before becoming a full-time healer is that I had a plan in place before permanently disembarking from the Borg collective and my corporate day job. My human side made a pact with spirit to do healing full-time only once my 401(k) reached $1 million. I have many friends working as full-time healers who quit their corporate jobs and struggled financially, and I was determined not to follow suit. However, circumstances in my job made it untenable to stay until the $1 million goal was met. There is a Yiddish saying, "We plan, God laughs." So, earlier than I had planned, God laughed, and I gave notice, which was a huge relief due to the untenable circumstances. In the weeks leading up to my resignation, I felt so much anxiety during my commute to work that no amount of grounding and breathwork would dissipate it completely. I knew with certainty that if I had stayed at the job, my health and self-confidence would have suffered. I had to be true to myself and have the self-awareness to know that I was no longer aligned with having a job and also working two jobs. I thought that must be what it felt like when people talk about the universe pushing you toward your life's calling.

The best way to commit to something scary or hard is to tell people so you can be accountable. I told my friends, co-workers, clients, and healing practice group that I was resigning from my day job, and everyone was extremely supportive. To my surprise, many wanted appointment slots as soon as my healing calendar opened up, which worked to alleviate one of my fears of not having enough clients.

Finally, I felt it was time to tell my mother about my very non-Korean-Borg plans to strike out as a full-time healer and leave my very Borg-approved corporate day job. My mom has lived her whole life in a fear-based state borne of the Collective, and as a result, raised me to rely on corporate jobs for security. I think God laughed again because she surprised me by saying, "Good. Now you're free."

CHAPTER

Walking Through Fear:
How I Stepped Out of
My Comfort Zone
By Linda Socker

Linda Socker has been inspiring people her whole life and is passionate about helping others. This comes from over twenty years as an Occupational Therapist working in hospitals, schools, and private practice. In 2004 after being introduced to Reiki and eventually becoming a Reiki Master/teacher, she experienced an "awakening," and her life changed dramatically. The shift in her perception of herself and the world was so profound she opened a Wellness Center to impact a greater number of people in need of healing.

Linda helps people discover their values and true purpose. She shows them how to move from pain and suffering to living their best life with health, fulfillment, and happiness. She specializes in using her healing gifts of energy therapies, craniosacral therapy, and spiritual mentoring. She is passionate about everything she does, providing loving, insightful, practical, and useful guidance to improve clarity, health, and inspiration for transformational change.

Linda has a BS in Occupational Therapy and Art Degree from Mount Mary University. She currently resides in Green Bay, Wisconsin. Her interests include spending time in nature, traveling, biking, ceramics, and spending time with her grandchild. Linda considers herself a lifelong learner and seeker of truth.

Contact information: Linda@Lindasocker.com

Chapter 15

Walking Through Fear

By Linda Socker

I GRADUATED FROM COLLEGE, married, had a career, and raised a family. A typical woman, you might say. At fifty-five, I suddenly found myself alone, paralyzed by fear, with no idea who I was. It was the darkest time of my life, and I didn't know how I would survive. I soon realized that fear had been a constant companion throughout my life, weaving in and out of experiences. With a partner beside me, I felt I could do anything. After several months of feeling despondent, I was faced with a choice to make: to sink or swim, knowing in my heart, I had to survive. I chose to make a commitment and embark on a quest to discover and know myself. I had nothing to lose.

To truly live a life I enjoy doing the things I love, I realized I needed to develop independence, learn to navigate and walk through fears, and take risks doing things I had never done before. *I chose to swim!* But first, I had to jump into the deep end and take control of my destiny. Over the next five years, I slowly began to heal, gradually ventured outside of my comfort zone, and planned solo adventures.

I discovered a newfound love for nature and the outdoors, especially during the summer. As I traveled to a favorite place in the Northwoods of Wisconsin, I frequently passed beautiful wooded state forest campgrounds, and all of a sudden, I yearned to go camping. When my kids were young, and when I was a child, I went camping. Every time I thought of going, I had the excuse. I didn't have a tent. Others told me, "Go buy a tent," when I shared my desire. I had a slew of excuses for why I couldn't, all of which were merely covers for the real reason. *Fear.* How could I go camping by myself? It's remarkable how fear can hold us back and prevent us from doing so many things in life. Fear is a choice, and I often chose fear, which stopped me cold.

"I want to go camping!" my inner child cried out for a second summer as I ventured through the Northwoods. I thought to myself, "This is insane!" I haven't gone camping in over twenty-six years! "Why do I want to go in the woods and sleep in a tent at the age of sixty?" I worked to convince myself that camping *is* a wonderful way to immerse myself in nature. Then I remembered that I didn't have a tent. As I continued with my excuses and justifications, my inner child kept speaking to me loud and clear and would not let up! Eventually, I had to listen and knew it was time to face fear and step out of my comfort zone. However, I lacked courage and could not follow through. Fear stopped me *again*.

For several weeks, I was intensely focused on meditation, meeting my Real Self, who has no fear. After experiencing emotional releases and new awarenesses, I vowed to listen to my inner child's needs and wants. I felt something shift within, and I was ready to make a bold move, take a risk, and embark on an adventure into the unknown. *I was ready to go camping!* I was astounded at my sudden bravery. "I can do this!" Everything unfolded beautifully! I quickly chose and purchased a tent, an inflatable mattress, a lantern, and a state park pass, and reserved a campsite. I hauled out the large, cobweb-covered camping bin buried in the garage corner and surveyed my gear. The day finally came! The car was packed and ready for the three-and-a-half-hour drive to Lake Wissota State Park, located on the border of Wisconsin and Minnesota. I was excited! I was going camping! I was ready for a much-needed quiet retreat to immerse myself in nature and explore. I had no idea what was in store for me or what adventures awaited. All the way there, I prayed. I knew Spirit was watching over me and would keep me safe. All I had to do was trust. Little did I know that my trust and faith were about to be tested.

The campground and surrounding area were so beautiful! After arriving at my campsite, it was time to pitch the tent. I had not done a trial setup but trusted I could erect the six-person tent by myself. I was right! Thank God the instructions had pictures! Within an hour, the tent was up. I stepped back and proudly regarded my accomplishment. I did it! After setting up camp, I explored the campground, built a fire, and cooked dinner. I was grateful to have learned how to start a fire as a Girl Scout. Sitting by the fire, I felt the peace and serenity of the woods, and my body relaxed. As I reflected, I recognized an absence of fear and felt fine being by myself. What an incredible feeling! After an evening by the fire and indulging on S'mores, it was time for bed.

Before I knew it, I woke up to a sunny, clear, blue sky and had survived the first night of camping in my new tent. Coffee! I needed coffee! Knowing I would not have electricity, I brought my coffeemaker invention. I inserted a coffee filter into a container I had cut holes in the bottom of, added coffee, and heated water from over the fire. *Viola! I had coffee!* After breakfast, I packed a lunch and headed out for the day, ready for my first adventure. I hopped on my bike, rode the few miles to the Ole Abe State Trail, and decided to head north.

Every five miles, there were small towns, and I stopped to explore. Along the route, I passed a woman with a small dog in a basket on the back of her bike, which made me smile. Another woman kindly gave me directions to the waterfalls. Thinking I needed a little air in my tires, I came across a gas station and filled them up. My destination was Brunet Island State Park. When I arrived, I stopped, ate my lunch, and waded into the lake to cool off. Then I headed home. It was a scorching day—90 degrees—so I drank plenty of water. Upon returning to the campsite, I discovered I had biked forty miles! I hadn't biked that far since high school! I was proud of myself. It had been a great day!

The next day, I took a break from biking. The beach was my choice of activity for the day, as well as exploring Chippewa Falls' quaint downtown area. Reflecting at the end of the day, I thought, "Wow, another great day!" I felt thrilled to have the courage to venture out and explore on my own.

Again, I was bold, having stepped out of my comfort zone and pleased with how my adventure was going.

On the third night, storms were on the horizon. I was awakened at two in the morning by weather sirens. Groggy from sleep, I checked my phone. Take shelter immediately; a severe weather warning with 60 mph winds and damaging hail. Expect damage to roofs, siding, and fallen trees-you know the drill. I chuckled to myself. *I'm in a tent!* I loaded my car with the essential belongings I didn't want to get wet and got in. "Where the hell is my phone?" I left it in the tent! At that moment, a torrential downpour started. Dashing back to the tent, I snatched up my phone and ran back to the car, completely drenched by the rain. On the campground map, I located a shelter about a mile away. I drove cautiously to the shelter, unable to see more than two feet in front of me. Thoughts were running through my mind: "Am I going to the right place?" "What are other people doing?" Yes, other cars were parked at the shelter when I got there. I wasn't alone, and I was safe. I laid back, closed my eyes, and listened to the rain. After about forty-five minutes, the rain subsided, and I returned to my campsite. All was well. The tent was still standing and dry inside. As I thought about the experience, I realized I had not been afraid. I instinctively knew what to do, remained calm, responded in the moment, and trusted that Spirit was with me to keep me safe. What a night! When on an adventure, you can never predict what will happen. I was tired, crawled into my sleeping bag, and fell asleep.

I woke to a quiet, serene morning with sunny skies. I was feeling relaxed, calm, and at peace. I wondered if I would camp again and, at that moment, thought I would. My morning routine in the woods was going smoothly. The fire was crackling, coffee was brewing, and muffins for breakfast were warming over the fire. After breakfast, I set out for another day of biking. I intended to go a shorter distance as it was another ninety-degree day, and my legs were still tired from the long ride I had done two days earlier. I was feeling empowered and bold as I embarked on another adventure. A leisurely and relaxing day was what I anticipated. I knew my intention for this experience was to walk through fear and prove to myself, "Yes, I can!" Today I chose to explore south on the trail.

I have gotten lost on trails a few times, so I have to rely on a map. As I biked, the trail was easy to follow. I felt confident I could find my way back. Even so, I was aware of the landmarks. It was a hot day, so I took my time and kept hydrated by drinking plenty of water. After biking five miles, I came upon a small park, an ideal place to stop and take a break. I enjoyed the lunch I had packed and relaxed by the lake to enjoy the scenery. Resuming my ride, I thought it would be fun to go to the zoo and chose to bike to Irvine Park and Zoo, only five miles away. Arriving at the zoo, I strolled to see the animals but soon noticed people carrying ice cream. Since it was a hot day, I wanted some! I found the ice cream shop, walked my bike to the window, and treated myself to Mackinaw Island fudge ice cream. With ice cream in one hand, I maneuvered my bike to a table and sat down to enjoy my special treat. Yummy!

After finishing my ice cream, I explored the park and ended up in a wildflower sanctuary. I parked my bike and sat on a bench to take in the beauty surrounding me. Butterflies and bees were flitting from flower to flower. As I watched them, I expressed gratitude for such an amazing day. Then, it was time to head back to the campground.

After biking for several miles, I came to a point where the trail went in several directions. I didn't know which way to go. A woman was walking, so I asked her for directions. She asked right away if I needed to rest, cool off from the heat, or get water, saying, "I live right there," as she pointed across the street to a condo. I told her, "Thank you, I'm fine, just staying hydrated and taking my time." Her name is Cindy. She was so kind! She pointed me in the direction of the highway. I was at the entrance to a nature preserve and wanted to explore. I checked my phone, and it appeared that the path connected to the trail along the highway, so I proceeded into the preserve. As I was riding, I was curious to know more about Cindy and wondered why I hadn't conversed with her more. Once again, I was stepping out of my comfort zone to engage with others. After biking about a mile, I realized it was not the correct path, so I turned around and headed back. I ran into Cindy again and had the opportunity to chat with her as she guided me to a parking lot. It was not the one where my car was. I thanked Cindy for her help, said goodbye, rode back to the preserve entrance, and traveled south on the trail along the highway. It was midday, the sun was beating down, and it was getting hotter.

After biking several miles, I saw a sign, Lake Hallie. This was not familiar. I checked my phone to see where I was and saw I had gone almost four miles the wrong way! How did this happen? The obvious choice was to turn around and head north. The hot sun was beating down on me, and I knew I had to stay hydrated. Then I heard a voice inside tell me to check the bag on my handlebars for my keys. I thought, "This is strange." Then I *heard* it again. For several weeks prior, I had been double-checking my bag for my keys. I stopped, unzipped my bag, and reached inside. My keys were not there! "How can this be? They have to be in here! Where are they? Oh, no. This can't be happening!" I've never lost my keys, much less while on vacation alone and miles from home. My mind instantly went into overdrive with an endless stream of thoughts and scenarios. I thought of passing out from heat exhaustion and being found on the sidewalk, burnt to a crisp, hitching a ride from someone with a pickup truck, being stranded for hours sitting next to my locked car, and calling my son-in-law, who was over two hours away, to come and rescue me. Those were a few of my thoughts, among others. The mind can cause so much trouble! What was I going to do? I had to stay calm! I was running low on water and could feel the heat getting to me. Suddenly, my old companion, fear, showed up. "No, go away!" As I struggled with fear, racing thoughts, thirst, and heat, I *knew* I had to stay calm and in the moment. I began to take deep breaths and quickly started talking to Spirit, asking for help. I *heard*, "Go to Cindy's house." I *knew* I had to get to Cindy's house, and she would help me. I pedaled the extra miles, retraced my path, and prayed to find my keys.

I got to what I hoped was Cindy's house, rang the doorbell, and she answered the door. Yes, I have the right house! I blurted out, "Hi, Cindy. I'm lost. I lost my keys, and I need help." She immediately invited me in and assured me everything would be fine. Her husband would be home soon and would know how to help. Refilling my water bottle, I chugged water to rehydrate. Cindy insisted I eat something and offered me chocolate chip cookies fresh from the oven. How could I resist? At that point, I was surprised at how calm I was. Intuitively, I knew everything would be okay. I just had to stay in the moment, respond to the next step in front of me, and trust! Yes, trust!

Cindy's husband arrived home, and we explained my predicament. I called Irvine Park and Zoo to inquire if any keys had been turned in. The woman who answered the phone said no, and told me the maintenance man could keep an eye out for my keys when he came through in the morning. That was not going to help me. I needed to find them today! Cindy offered to drive me to the places I had stopped. We got in her car and drove to the park. Thoughts started racing in again. There was no way to retrace my route on my bike, and vehicles could not drive on the trail. What was I going to do? We pulled into the first park I had stopped at, and there were no keys. One more place to try. I continued to breathe and pray.

On the way to the park and zoo, I called the police department. The police always help. The receptionist answered, and I explained my situation. She suggested I contact a locksmith to unlock my car. She didn't seem to understand that I didn't have my keys, so getting my car unlocked would not help. She put me on hold to speak to a detective. While on hold, we arrived at the park and zoo. I went inside the building where I had purchased ice cream. The man who had waited on me came forward, and I asked him if anyone had turned in a set of keys. He strolled over to the lost-and-found box and reached in. As he pulled his hand out, I recognized Minnie Mouse dangling from the key ring. I said, "Oh, my God! Those are my keys!" I was so relieved and thankful! Someone found them near the table where I sat to eat ice cream and turned them in.

Cindy drove me to the parking lot where my car was. In the meantime, her husband had put my bike in his car and came to meet us. I lifted the bike onto my bike rack and profusely thanked Cindy and her husband. Feeling tremendous relief and gratitude, I drove back to the campsite. What a day! Never having lost my keys before, and having the experience while on vacation alone was frightening! I knew there was a valuable lesson in it for me. When I discovered my keys were missing, I immediately gave it over to Spirit and asked for help. This experience was a test of faith. I had to trust that I would be all right no matter what happened, keys or no keys. I recalled how Cindy was put in my path and just so happened to show me where she lived, which enabled me to go to her house for help. I knew I had to get to her home and knew she would help me. I also knew I had to remain calm, stay in the moment, respond to what was in front of me, and not let my mind race into the future.

There are good people in the world, and I met two of them that day. Cindy and her husband were my angels. They were so kind, letting a stranger into their house, and they went above and beyond to help me. Their calm demeanor helped me stay calm. Cindy also makes the best chocolate chip cookies.

This experience confirmed that Spirit is looking after me. All I have to do is ask for help, trust, and have faith. This camping trip was a retreat to get to know more about me! It's exciting to get to know more about who I truly am at my age. I can be bold, step out of my comfort zone, and walk through fear. I am capable of anything, and I know I am the only one holding me back. I also know I am never truly alone.

I've recently discovered that nothing is really lost. I just can't find it in that moment. I've lost many things, but more important are the things I have found.

Whenever you lose an object, visualize it in your hand. If you find yourself in a difficult situation, I invite you to pause, take slow, deep breaths, stay in the moment, ask for help, and trust that you will be shown the way. I found myself in frightening circumstances that tested my faith. Everything unfolded as it was meant to. This adventure deepened my trust and faith. Fear is a choice, and I chose to walk through it only to confirm fear is false. I'm looking forward to more solo adventures to get to know myself better. I have become much more courageous and have emerged a much bolder woman.

The Shadow In The Night

Fear comes out of nowhere
Like a shadow in the night,
Creeping in so subtly
And filling me with fright.

Wanting to move forward
With things I aspire to do,
Fear stops me in my tracks
As it lingers through and through.

I choose to live life fully
And simply want to play.
It's time to walk through fear
You will show me the way.

I muster up my courage
And activate my will,
Step out of my comfort zone
To do the things that thrill.

I'm going to be bold!
It's time for me to soar.
I push fear aside
"You don't belong here anymore!"

Suddenly I notice
The fear has gone away.
I've conquered the false
I'm ready now to play.

With fear no longer present
And courage in its place,
I see all my potential
And a smile comes to my face.

I plan the new adventures
Step out into the light,
To do as I am meant
Without the shadow in the night.

Fear no longer stops me
Trusting is the key.
Spirit walks beside me
And now I am free.

CHAPTER

Sixteen

Blend and Ascend:
My Four Catalysts for
Taking Bold Action
By Janet Zavala

Janet Zavala is a best-selling writer and coach. She is passionate about making proven self-empowerment techniques accessible to a greater number of people. She is a contributor to the internationally best-selling book *Own Your Awesome*, available on Amazon and author of *The Nature of Transformation, A Comprehensive Life Coaching System, Inspired by Nature, to Heal Your Body, Mind, and Spirit*, being released in 2023.

Janet holds a bachelor's degree and coaching certification. As a thirty-year veteran of corporate America, she led her department's women's empowerment group, providing thought leadership and strategic guidance in the development of more than thirty events delivered to over 700 employees, focused on personal and professional development.

Janet maintains a blog that can be found on her website at JanetZavalaCoaching.com. You can find her on all social media channels.

Join Janet's Facebook group community at *Living Intentionally*, where conversations are centered around helping people achieve their goals and dreams.

Janet currently offers one-on-one life coaching sessions and interactive group sessions. Janet helps her clients navigate a variety of personal issues, using her intuitive abilities and compassionate approach to help them transform and live their best lives.

Chapter 16

Blend and Ascend

By Janet Zavala

O NE OF MY EARLIEST memories was riding in the passenger seat of my mom's car in a state of total confusion. At four, I was having what were the first of hundreds, maybe thousands, of existential crises. My inner dialogue was debating how I ended up in my body and this existence. Why was I riding in this car, with this lady as my mother, instead of the car next to us at the red light? I could not understand why I wasn't able to select the experiences of someone else in the moment. How did I get stuck with this family? What if I wanted to change? I thought I should be able to switch realities with others whenever I felt like it. At such an early age, I already felt like I didn't belong in my life. I remember feeling out of place and trapped.

I now know that these feelings were the likely remnants of a past life as I was settling into the new one. I believe, as Dr. Brian Weiss speaks about in his book *Many Lives, Many Masters*, you choose your next life. You choose the experiences that will elevate your soul. I clearly had not settled into the decision I had made to live my life.

As the years went on, the experiences of my youth did not give me comfort of my life selection, nor did the years eliminate my existential questioning. I was the last of four kids, five years younger than my closest sibling. I was not planned or wanted. I was left with the understanding that not only was I an accident, but I also added a couple of years onto a decaying marriage. A dysfunctional home life, being kidnapped by my mother at the age of nine and changing schools five times in the span of about two years reaffirmed my belief that I did not fit anywhere.

My teenage years did not bring any more assurance that I fit in when fitting in really matters most. You're assuming everyone else feels like they fit in because, well, they act like it. I did not possess any obvious gift, interest, or skill that would allow me to join a clique naturally. I was too afraid to be bad and not good enough to excel. This put me squarely in the invisible middle. My anxiety and introverted nature had me avoiding anything that would bring me unwanted attention. My survival strategy was to blend. My plan was to disappear and not stand out. I tried hard not to stand out in a good way and certainly not in a bad way. Blend and survive was my life strategy throughout high school. But once out, I started making calculated bold choices.

I don't view myself as particularly bold. I am logical, careful, and strategic. I plan my life three steps ahead. I desire a safety net, but I have always had to weave this net by myself. I craft it, so I don't fall beyond the point of no return. Far too often, I'm strategizing and weaving during a freefall.

When boldness was required, I took the steps necessary to improve and elevate my life. I've been bold in pursuing my own healing. I have been relentlessly focused on ascending the experiences and trauma that I apparently chose to have to build the kind of life that I knew I could have.

There have been four major catalysts for bold action that have transformed me and guided my ascension. These circumstances propelled me into action. I've never been bold for bold's sake. These actions have been purposeful. During these pivotal times, I evaluated if staying in *this* place with all its comfortable discomfort or trying *that* so I could ascend my current circumstances was the best option. There is an undeniable feeling when you know bold action is required. It's a crossroads where the choice is staying stuck in a life you don't want or taking a chance to build a life you desire.

Catalyst #1 – A bold move to avoid a narrow existence

Have you ever felt like you fell into life? You did not travel there, nor did you choose the destination. To your surprise, you may even realize you're not choosing the next turn, either. This is exactly how I was beginning to feel during my senior year of high school. My part-time job at a bank quickly turned into a full-time gig as soon as I grabbed that diploma. A year into this undefined life, I realized the road ahead seemed narrow and wildly unfulfilling. I had no idea how I wanted my life to look. I wasn't shown by example that you could have dreams and create your own life. My examples were more of accidental living versus intentional design. Life, I thought, was something that happened to you, not created by you.

One year after graduation and one solid year into the mundane life I'd eked out for myself, my high school friend announced that she was leaving our small mid-western town to live with her aunt in San Diego. There was not an ounce of hesitation when she asked if I wanted to join her on the drive cross country. I would finally go home to California after leaving when I was nine years old. The beautiful and scary thing about being nineteen, if you're lucky, is that you have no concept of certain dangers in life. I'd experienced trauma, but I maintained a cloak of privilege that is not afforded to everyone.

Within two weeks, I quit the bank and planned our cross-country road trip. I spent exactly zero time regretting my decision or thinking about alternatives.

Two 19-year-old girls hit the road; her in her car, me in my new car, a recently purchased Honda Civic stick shift. What better way to learn how to drive a stick shift, I thought, than while driving from Illinois to California? I would be taking with me a new car payment while being unemployed. As I said, I had no second thoughts and zero regrets. I would figure it out. I'd start weaving when I got to California.

Approximately 550 miles and less than 9 hours into a 2,000-mile trek, my friend's car stalled out in a barren crossroads with one gas station in the middle of nowhere on the border of Oklahoma and Arkansas. We sat at an intersection with a flat brown landscape in each of the four directions. It looked like a scene from a movie where the devil shows up with an offer you can't refuse. But this was no movie, and I do not play the blues guitar. And the only person who would hopefully show up was the UPS driver with the needed car part.

After two days of sitting in a gas station with nothing but a kid named Turkey to keep us entertained, the mystery car part arrived. We were on our way again – for a few hours, anyway. Her car broke down again. This time in the more populated town of Muskogee, Oklahoma. We spent two more weeks waiting for the car to be fixed. At least we had a Walmart and a movie theater to slightly avoid insanity and killing each other out of frustration, boredom, and competing soap opera preferences.

It would have been easy to backtrack, once we were able, back to the safety of our maternal homes. Even though we each spent more of our savings than we intended, the option to go back wasn't discussed. Neither of us wanted the safe life that waited for us back in our small town.

It's easier when you're younger to make life-altering bold choices. You have fewer obligations and fears. But I know for the two of us to have made that bold choice, there were countless others who chose to stay in that small town. We did not see a place for us in that world that didn't end with disappointment at best or reliving the dysfunctions of our families at worst. We were emboldened by our youth and the possibilities of what life could be.

"My friends from high school

Married their high school boyfriends

Moved into houses

In the same ZIP codes where their parents live

But I, I could never follow"

The Long Way Around. The Chicks. Natalie Maines, Martie Maguire, Emily Erwin with Daniel Dodd Wilson

Catalyst #2 – Being bold to step into my potential

Once I arrived at my sister's condo after the two-week road trip, I needed to quickly find a job. I had a $232 car payment, and for the first time in my life, I had rent to pay. An employment agency quickly set me up for three interviews. Going to the first, I got lost on the confusing California freeways. Pre-cell phones and navigation, I cried into a pay phone, telling the agency I couldn't do the interview. The next one, I went to in my smartest business attire, a black skirt and a black and red striped blouse (it was the 80s, don't judge). I aced the interview, even after they said I'd likely be standing and filing all day. I enthusiastically told them that I would absolutely love that. As the interview neared its conclusion, I was told it was "probably ok" what I was wearing however they preferred that the clothing I wore not be so bold.

The third and final interview was at an office/ware-house-type business. They were moving into this new space in Orange County from downtown Los Angeles. An ultimately sweet but scary at first office manager with thick black eyeliner interviewed me. I received offers for both. I chose the more relaxed office/warehouse. I would be the eager new receptionist.

They hired a lot of new people to work in this new office. We were all getting to know each other for the first time in this new space. I quickly became bored just answering the phones. One of the ways I counteracted boredom was to find new and quicker ways of doing things. I started to stand out. People noticed and began giving me extra assignments. This got me my first promotion to the accounting department.

As new positions and opportunities came up, I was always available. I took all the promotions offered. I kept on increasing my skillset, knowledge, and credibility with the organization. Being bold to take on extra work and excelling gave me the increased confidence I sorely needed. I enjoyed feeling valuable and relied upon. I didn't let fear keep me from accepting new roles with increased responsibility.

I also didn't let my inability to set healthy boundaries and not being an advocate for myself prevent me from walking away from that job 11 years later. When my value was abused, and I was working 60–80-hour work weeks for years, I boldly left this place that had become like a second family. Not having another job to go to didn't prevent me from walking away and taking the next nine months off to recover. I became a room mother for my son's second-grade class and started weaving again.

Even though the experience ended the way it did, I wouldn't have the opportunities I have today without allowing myself to stand out and stepping into my ambition while learning to apply my natural critical thinking skills and ability to problem solve. These skills served me well all these years.

Catalyst #3 – Being bold to establish roots

My childhood years were traumatic. My early adult life was chaotic. I longed for a strong foundation. I craved solid ground for my son and me to feel safe. I did not want him to experience the instability I felt.

We were living in our two-bedroom rental house during the housing crisis in 2008. I was working at my new corporate job and doing well. I was in the middle of separating from my husband. For cheap fun, we would tour open houses. I toured a huge house on the hill that, even during the housing crisis with reduced pricing, was far out of range. In actuality, I never dreamed that buying a house could be a reality. That's when an ambitious broker and real estate agent assured me that I would easily qualify.

Could I even dream of buying a home on my own? When I allowed the possibility of home ownership to enter my brain as a real possibility, we began touring all conditions of homes. People were losing their homes in record numbers, and one apparent strategy to release anger was to destroy the home they were vacating. After seeing many, we found *the one*. I told the agent I didn't want a swimming pool. It had a pool. Two of the kitchen cabinets had been ripped out. It looked like they were in the middle of home renovations when their loan likely became upside down. Some things were brand new, like the windows and floors. Some things needed a lot of work, like the garage door, bathroom, and kitchen cabinets. It had, as they say, good bones.

My son and I felt it. It was ours. I know they say you're not supposed to get emotionally attached, but why wouldn't you want to feel a strong connection in the place you're going to call home? It had a huge Jacaranda tree in the front yard that was in full bloom. My first home, my dad's home, had a Jacaranda tree. The Jacaranda tree's spiritual message is one of wisdom and rebirth. It felt like it was meant to be.

There were multiple bids. The agent told us to be bold in our offer. I was, and we got it. We would have our forever home. But not so fast. As mentioned, I was ending my marriage. It's amazing the things you learn buying a house. Did you know you cannot buy a home by yourself if you're married without the spouse signing off on having ownership or responsibility for the house? Well, this turn of events was a problem. You see, my now ex-husband was, as they would say in New Jersey, "away." It would take multiple attempts and me paying extra for a notary to drive ninety miles north to get his signature on the paperwork.

I was not deterred. I was hell-bent on ascending this circumstance of my life. I needed that safe haven. I felt transient until I was able to secure this grounding and healing place. It has been the sanctuary where I healed from my trauma, nestled in the sense of security I have only been able to find there.

Catalyst #4 – Being bold for my passions

I was struck by what a colleague said to me when I was excitingly telling her about the recently published best-selling compilation book I participated in: *Own Your Awesome and Step into Your Authenticity*. I told her about my ambitions to participate in more of these types of projects as well as publish my own book. We also spoke about my desire to expand my life coaching business. She said that she wished more people would talk about what they are passionate about and what they are doing outside of their day jobs. My colleague said she wished others were bold enough to talk about their passions so openly.

Now you must understand how unusual these conversations are in the corporate world. People bring only a small percentage of their true selves into the work environment. There is an unwritten doctrine that implies that we should not express our interests outside of work unless it is closely tied to the work we do. The assumption is you will be passed over for jobs, thought of as a risk of leaving, or that you are not 100% dedicated to the job you have.

The other thing that corporate America does is wrap you in this cocoon of a steady income and benefits. They dangle in front of you the prospect of advancement and raises (and more work), These opportunities can be difficult to acquire, so we jump at the opportunities presented, often deferring our true passions.

I'm not saying that a corporate career and climbing that exhausting ladder cannot be fulfilling to many. But I am saying that very few people can say they are passionate about what they do. Enjoying your job and the fruits of your labor do not often equate to passionate living.

I was a good twenty years into my corporate career when I discovered my passion for coaching. Coaching led me to write. These are the things that I'm passionate about. Unfortunately, corporate obligations can often lead you to deprioritize (a corporate word) your passions.

In 2017 I was successfully putting my passions aside due to a demanding but enjoyable role. I was able to infuse coaching activities to make them fulfilling enough when they dangled a promotion in front of me. I sought the council of executives and was encouraged (basically directed) to take the promotion "for my own development." That began what were the worst 18 months of my career. I walked into a toxic environment; the toxicity swirled around me and then spit me out. I ultimately landed somewhere safer and better for my mental health. After my mental health recovered enough to think straight, I realized I had put my passions on hold for far too long.

My passion for coaching and writing was sitting dusty on the shelf. When we enter survival mode, the energy needed to dedicate to passion projects is diminished, if not totally zapped. In challenging situations, I search for the lessons I'm meant to learn. When I catch my breath, I find the opportunity to grow and ascend. Many times, challenging situations happen as the universe's way of redirecting your attention.

The universe orchestrated these events on my behalf, although incredibly painful and stressful. I had been lulled into the comfort of a satisfying role that kept me from going all in on my dreams and passions. She dangled the opportunity for advancement, which was the wrong opportunity at the wrong place, time, and people.

That experience required me to define what it was I genuinely wanted to do with my career. Now I boldly and fiercely pursue my dreams. I talk about them with other people. I announced myself as a life coach and a writer first, whereas I used to respond with my corporate role when people asked what I did.

Taking bold action does not mean being reckless. Bold is different from courage and confidence. Bold is being afraid and still taking a chance. Bold is traveling your life's journey on your terms. Being bold means that you have the strength to make choices for your highest good. Boldness includes being able to identify and pursue your passions, even in the face of objections and obstacles. Being bold means that you are unapologetically goal-oriented and motivated, ready to face and overcome the fear and self-doubt that will undoubtedly show up. Traveling the road less traveled and listening to your intuition is boldness personified.

What helped me to take bold action were tenacity, patience, and an unflinching desire to improve the quality of my life. Throughout my life, I would blend in when I needed to survive, but I understood when it was time to ascend and step out of the mold. Ascending from a life that you did not

design to one that you create with intention is the ultimate
act of boldness.

Journal Prompts

Use these journal prompts to celebrate where you have
been bold in your life and challenge what may be holding
you back from taking action necessary to intentionally design the life you want.

Describe a time when you took bold action to change the
trajectory of your life. When I started thinking about what
I would write in this chapter, I was convinced that I had
not done a single bold thing in my life. Upon reflection, I
can accept and acknowledge that I have been incredibly
bold. This has provided me with increased confidence and
motivation to continue to pursue my dreams.

- What was the catalyst that led you to take these bold
  actions?

- What lessons did you learn about yourself, about
  others, or about life through the process?

If you have struggled with taking bold action to improve
your life, list everything that's holding you back.

- Do you struggle with being too self-critical? Do you
  doubt your decision-making? Do you fear you will
  upset others? List all your barriers.

- Ask yourself if the assumptions you identified that
  prevent you from taking action are true. What is the
  evidence that proves they are true? What evidence

(past experience) do you have that your assumptions are false?

- If you still believe these assumptions to be true, what action can you take to move past these barriers? Perhaps the next right action is doing some research, having a conversation, or strategizing on the appropriate steps that feel right for you. One small action in the right direction will produce more action over time.

What are the long-term risks of not taking bold action to elevate your life?

What are the long-term possibilities of taking bold action to elevate your life? What is the potential of what you can become or achieve?

Made in United States
North Haven, CT
06 February 2023

32133705R00124